Bath

Marrekesh

Tamanresset

Agadez

Kano

Yaounde

Kribi

Bangui

Kisangani

Kigali

Dar es Salaam

Lusaka

Blantyre

Victoria Falls

Bulawago

Johannesburg

Durban

Cape Town

RIDING
AFRICA

MICHAEL HOWARD-KYAN

The Book Guild Ltd

First published in Great Britain in 2021 by
The Book Guild Ltd
9 Priory Business Park
Wistow Road, Kibworth
Leicestershire, LE8 0RX
Freephone: 0800 999 2982
www.bookguild.co.uk
Email: info@bookguild.co.uk
Twitter: @bookguild

Typeset in 12pt Minion Pro

Printed and bound in the UK by TJ Books LTD, Padstow, Cornwall

ISBN 978 1913551 865

British Library Cataloguing in Publication Data.
A catalogue record for this book is available from the British Library.

© Michelin et Cie, 2011, Authorisation No. GB26082020

TO TRISH

IN GRATITUDE OF THIRTY-THREE YEARS
OF UNFAILING LOVE AND SUPPORT

"All men dream but not equally. Those who dream at night in the dusty recesses of their minds wake in the day to find that it was vanity, but the dreamers of the day are dangerous men for they may act their dream with open eyes to make it possible."

Introduction from Seven Pillars of Wisdom
T.E. Lawrence

Chapter 1

THE IDEA

Many years ago, well nearly forty, I had a dream of an idea to undertake an exciting adventure.

I could think of nothing else once the audacious idea came to me that it would be brilliant to try and ride my five-year-old motorcycle across the continent of Africa leaving behind my family, friends and established career in favour of the open road. It was January 1981, I was a twenty-five-year-old newly qualified and looking for adventure.

I knew I wanted to be on my way by early spring, which meant I had little time to prepare for the trip. That in itself was another challenge.

For the last two years I'd been working in London for a small West End firm of Chartered Surveyors and had completed my qualification period. Suddenly, May was looming up all too soon and my life became a mad scramble to get 101 things sorted out in time. The things to be done roughly fell into three heads: myself (visas, vaccinations, etc.), the bike (documents, spare parts, etc.) and equipment.

Fortunately, my work in London took me daily within easy reach of most embassies so if a visa was possible to obtain it was not too demanding to pop in and fill in the necessary forms, invariably in quadruplicate, and leave the passport and photos until the visa was issued usually two days later.

One of the most difficult of these to get was the Nigerian one. The staff at the consulate demanded to see £30 of travellers' cheques for every day of stay. The embassy of Zaire announced that the only visa they could issue was for entry via Kinshasa, the capital, completely off my route and probably impossible to reach overland in any event. This visa I would have to try and pick up elsewhere en route.

Thomas Cook's health centre in the West End was most helpful with general medical advice, vaccinations for cholera, yellow fever and a host of other infectious diseases. They also insisted that I carried a certificate confirming that I had not been in contact with any person suffering from smallpox despite no cases of smallpox having been reported anywhere in the world in the previous four years, a wonderful success story for the UN and mankind.

Chapter 2

PREPARATIONS

A BOOK HAD RECENTLY COME OUT CALLED *JUPITER'S TRAVELS* BY A FORMER *Sunday Times* journalist, Ted Simon. I purchased a copy and studied it intensively; it was a great read and very useful in providing me with ideas of spares and kit worth taking. Worth its weight in gold was an air pump which could be run by removing one of my spark plugs, screwing it into the cylinder and firing the engine on the other cylinder to operate. Also, a small camping stove fuelled by petrol was to be a godsend, neither of which I would have thought of.

I was living in West Kensington and I thought it would be worthwhile going to the motorcycle exhibition at Earl's Court where coincidently Ted Simon had a stand to promote his new book.

I met with him but I don't think he believed that I was genuine in my plan to ride across Africa on a two-stroke Suzuki as he expressed not a great amount of interest in me other than trying to get me to buy another copy of his book!

Also at the exhibition I started asking around the various exhibitors as to who might be able to make up the largest fuel tank possible for a Suzuki GT 250, as I realised that with a fuel consumption of less than thirty miles to the gallon and a current capacity of just over three gallons this would not get me very far. I eventually found an exhibitor displaying racing motorcycles with very large aluminium fuel tanks. The exhibitor was a guy called Tony Huck from a firm called Maitland Racing and he expressed great interest in my project and agreed there and then to have a crack at making the largest fuel tank ever fitted to a GT 250. Parting with £120 two weeks later, my bike now had a stunning shaped polished aluminium tank which could hold over seven gallons of precious fuel.

I later managed to pick up a rectangular speedboat fuel container with another five-gallon capacity, which fitted inside the rear top box that I had fitted to the bike back in my student days at Bristol to carry my books and sandwiches. Overall my range was now extended from 100 miles to well over 300 miles.

I spent a small fortune on portable spares such as gaskets, oil seals, plugs, pistons, rings, cables, etc., most of which it turned out I was still to have with me unused 28,000km later in Cape Town. Remarkably some of these items were very useful in the 2018 restoration of Suzy.

A few days before leaving London I put the bike in for its annual MOT; to my great surprise it was failed, supposedly on the issue of steering bearings. Oh well, no time for a fix and a retest so the whole trip across Africa was undertaken on an MOT failure. In 2018 when we rebuilt the machine, we found nothing at all wrong with these bearings and indeed reused them, so it seems to me it was an attempt at a con!

I stopped work at Easter 1981 and moved my parents' home in Bath. On the M4 heading west at speed I had the curious sensation of my rear wheel trying to overtake my front wheel on the left-hand side; easing off the throttle the wheel then tried to move to the right-hand side; it was my first ever blowout. As I waited on the hard shoulder after calling the AA from the roadside assist box a group of a dozen Hells Angels came to a halt by me. Feeling somewhat intimidated and nervous I did my best to remain outwardly calm. They were very interested in my tank adaptation to the bike, which had made them decide to stop, and were sincere in offers to help. However, they departed fairly soon with a roar that only a bunch of chopped Triumphs and Harleys can produce after I told them that help was already on the way.

Spending the next two weeks making final preparations, I bought a throw-over double saddle bag, a large tank bag with clear plastic map holder and a pair of ex-army hessian bags to go on either side of the fuel tank.

Overall, I had rigged the bike to carry a huge amount of stuff, far more than was necessary, but I figured that better too much than too little.

Now that things were beginning to come into order, I decided to contact an acquaintance working for Oxfam to see if they would be interested in using the trip to raise funds for a deserving cause. Personally, I felt that it would be satisfying to feel that others would benefit from my trip. My contact was most enthusiastic about this proposal and we agreed that any money raised would go for the treatment of leprosy in Africa.

To me it was even in the 1980s a total anachronism that leprosy in Africa should exist on the appalling scale which it did, in a supposedly modern and developing world. All the more so when I learned that proven treatment techniques and preventative drugs had been available for use since the late 1940s and are cheap to produce.

The disease is particularly widespread in Africa and Asia where a great many sufferers are often unaware of the existence of treatment or indeed if aware are unable to obtain it. Often at first, they hide the disease from their family and friends, covering up the light patches of skin lesions as they appear. When their horrendous secret is discovered they are often cast out of home and community to beg or starve and to always keep their distance.

People with leprosy are very susceptible to infection of wounds for the disease often means a loss of sensation. It is often the case that a cut or a thorn in the sole of the foot for example goes unnoticed and unattended as nervous and muscular tissue is preyed upon by the bacilli, so disfigurement leads to loss of fingers, toes, bridge of nose and most terrifying of all, the paralysis of eyelids, making the patient unable to shut his eyes or blink at all so that the all-important lubrication of the surface of the eyeball is dried up causing it to become opaque and resulting in blindness.

I make no apology for this graphic account of the "living death" for I feel that generally people in our Western world are all too often completely unaware of what precisely leprosy does to its victims and also of the fact that it is very much a real disease challenging mankind as indeed smallpox used to. If leprosy was closer to the doorstep of Europe people would be more aware of what the condition is and inevitably more attention would be given towards its prevention and cure.

Chapter 3

LEAVING

O XFAM PRODUCED AN APPALLING "SHOCKING GREEN" PRESS RELEASE WHICH, IN view of the rapidly approaching departure date now set for May 1st, I had to accept rather than opt for a less lurid and more accurate introduction to the press; however, the colour did the trick and within a day or two of circulation I was being hunted down by all manner of local publications and radio stations.

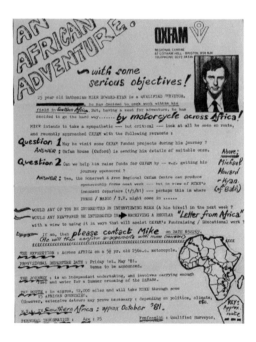

Oxfam publicity sheet

I also thought it might be prudent to try the bike out in sandy conditions so made a fairly long ride over to Brean Sands on the Bristol Channel where it was possible to ride down on to the beach and ride up and down it a fair way. I discovered pretty sluggish behaviour in the thicker dry sand at the top of the beachhead but reasonable traction where the sand was damp and firm, not particularly good news. On my return home the phone went with no warning and I was talking live to Radio Bristol about my plans.

A leaving ceremony was organised by Oxfam and to his credit Chris Patten MP for Bath agreed to officiate at the taking leave ceremony from St John's RC church in Bath. I remember his words of encouragement as being "One bloody good bump and the whole lot will fly off I should imagine!"

Suddenly it was all over and I found myself alone bowling out through the green valleys with a curious mixture of emotions: sadness at leaving my beautiful home and those I loved but also a strong exhilaration, almost unknown by me before, of breaking free with the whole world in front of me. What an adventure!

(Note from diary – odometer reading 24,582 at start.)

With an intoxicating smell of freedom in my nostrils I soon picked up the rhythm of my heavily laden machine. At low speed it would develop a gentle wobble, but this would disappear over 30mph and with surprise I found that I could even accelerate up to 60mph. Before leaving I had not taken the opportunity to do any trial runs on a fully loaded basis spending the last few days instead focused on last-minute preparations and buying necessities.

So involved was I with this first ride that I overshot Oxford by thirty miles, touring Reading en route, and I had forgotten to take a road map of England with me.

When eventually I arrived at Oxford to spend the night prearranged with my brother Paul and his charming wife Karen, we realised that my machine was grossly overloaded and later that evening we unpacked and ran through virtually everything leaving out dozens of hopefully unnecessary items.

Next morning, I took the London road feeling much lighter and more confident of my ability to handle the machine without assistance than before, when it had been all but impossible for me to put the bike on its main stand without help.

My next appointment, which I was really looking forward to, was a lunchtime rendezvous at the Colton Arms in W14 with some London friends who were probably convinced by this time that I had a wire loose.

After a couple of farewell pints, I was once more pushing my way across the familiar streets of London, across Blackheath Common, on to the Dover road and on down to Kent.

Bath Evening Chronicle photo shoot before departure

Leaving Bath send-off by Canon Kelly and Chris Patten (then MP for Bath)

Bike overloaded and ready to go from home

Bike overloaded and ready to go from home

Bath and West

Evening Chronicle

CITY

FRIDAY, MAY 1, 1981 — 10p

Carpets!
WE MEASURE & ESTIMATE
FREE
ALL CARPETS FITTED BY
OUR OWN EXPERT FITTERS
HAYES

CIRCLES
"... to round off your appetite"
Jollys
Milsom Street, Bath. Tel: 62911

BOBBIES DEMAND: CRACK DOWN ON RIOTS

POLICE TODAY CALLED for more equipment and better support after the "outrages" of the Bristol and Brixton riots.

The riots have added a new dimension to the problem of violence against the police, and the casualty rate is now totally unacceptable, said the Police Federation.

Mike Howard-Kyan with Canon Kelly and MP Mr Chris Patten outside St John's Church, North Parade.

A statement issued following a meeting of the federation's joint central committee said, "We believe that over this same period, society has failed to recognise the dangers for itself of not responding with adequate strength and severity to outbreaks of this kind.

"The feeling has grown up among people who take part in mass gatherings and either assault police officers, or attack other citizens and wilfully damage property, that they stand a chance of escaping scot-free with conduct because of the anonymity of crowds, and that even if they are caught, the punishments inflicted will not be sufficiently severe to deter them and others from repeating such conduct."

The statement continued, "The casualty rate among our members has become totally unacceptable. Too many police officers are being asked to face mobs while wearing ordinary police uniform and have virtually no defence against missiles and even petrol bombs.

"We now call upon the Home Secretary, as a first priority, to ensure that all police officers, when ordered to deal with riots and disorder, are wearing headgear which is capable of withstanding a blow from a missile and which protects the face, and have sufficient protection to avoid the risk of serious injury to other parts of the body."

12,000 mile trek

BATH SURVEYOR Mike Howard-Kyan set off for a 12,000 mile trek across Africa today with a blessing from Canon James Kelly, of St John's Church, North Parade.

On his heavily laden, specially adapted 250cc Suzuki, Mike, 35, of 139 Church Road, Combe Down, pulled away on the first stage of his journey.

He will cross France before starting on the hardest part of his trip, 12,000 miles through 13 countries from Morocco to Botswana. He will even attempt to cross the Sahara Desert — 2,500 miles in summer — and

should reach his destination in October.

Mike is paying for the trip himself, but Oxfam is arranging sponsorship, with all proceeds going towards leprosy projects in Africa.

Sponsorship forms are available from Oxfam at 63 Cotham Hill, Bristol.

Bath MP Chris Patten and representatives of other political parties were there at the send-off.

Their Green Goddess of love

THE FIREMEN'S STRIKE of 1977 was a grim time for many people — and the pressure was very hard on the men who worked the Green Goddess fire tenders which were brought out of mothballs to deal with the emergency.

But for Senior Aircraftsman Mick Williams, on detachment at the TA Centre in Upper Bristol Road, Bath, it was the start of a romance. While he was working on the Goddess he met a young section officer in the Girls' Venture Corps, and tomorrow they will marry at St Mary's Roman Catholic Church, Julian Road, Bath.

"I wasn't love at first sight," the bride, 21-year-old Kim Penfield, said today. "I didn't agree to go out with him straight away, but after I'd come back from a holiday in Italy he was still around."

"Then my parents invited him for Christmas dinner because they felt sorry for him. He was on duty at the TA Centre on Christmas Day, and it was the turn of the officers to serve the airmen.

"But the fire alarm went off when they had just started serving the soup, so he didn't get his Christmas dinner. My parents invited him back here and that was when the romance really started."

The Girls' Venture Corps, which does similar work to the Air Training Corps, played an important part during the firemen's strike in helping the Green Goddess drivers. Kim, a dental surgery assistant, is still a keen member and girls from the Corps will provide a fanfare and guard of honour outside the church tomorrow.

Mick, 22, comes from Coventry and is stationed at Brandy, Dyfed.

They have one problem to be resolved — that of rank. "He is supposed to salute me when we meet, because I'm an officer!" said Kim.

Secret talks on new spa building deal

A POSSIBLE PROPERTY deal was discussed at a private meeting between senior Bath councillors and spa consortium chief Lord Selsdon this week.

It could involve the city and other property owners contributing buildings towards the consortium's ambitious £35m scheme to re-open Bath's spa.

Chief executive Mr David Beeton said today: "Lord Selsdon explained what involvement would be needed by the council to progress the scheme further."

But he refused to give any more details.

So far the city council's sub-committee has authorised a study which has now been completed.

But while they wait for Green Park Station to be Sainsbury's, it was agreed to set aside £480,000 to provide new swimming facilities, if possible, in spa water.

The meeting was attended by Mr Laurie Coombs, Mr Tony Rhymes and Mr Howard Routledge, Tory chairman of the spa.

Mr Coombs said the meeting was to discuss the presentation of the scheme at a special meeting open to the public at the Pump Room on May 18.

"Lord Selsdon obviously wants the best deal he can and we've got for a long while the best deal for Bath. A lot of money is going to be involved but we were not asked for a further contribution at this stage." he said.

Bath woman's £62,441

MRS EDITH Emily Furze of 183, Hansford Square, Bath, left estate valued at £62,110 gross, £61,441.

Mrs Furze, a member of the Bath restaurant family, whose husband, Mr Bramwell Furze, died in 1942, has left £100 to Southstoke Evangelical Free Church, of

which she was a member for many years.

Her son, Mr David Furze, who now runs the family restaurant business in Cheap Street, is the executor at the church.

Probate has been granted to Louisa D. King, of 4, Hansford Close, Combe Down, Bath.

In the bag for a special delivery

FOUR BATH University students were sacked at the city's post sorting office today — all for charity.

The four — pictured here getting stamped on by chief postal inspector Mr Ted Hammond — were tied up in mail bags and wheeled to Bath Spa railway station to meet a High Speed Train.

The exercise was a dry run for Sunday, when they will be "posted" to Warrington, Cheshire courtesy of the Post Office and British Rail.

The four, student union president Ian Ross, 23, and 19-year-old first year students Justin Morris, Harry Harding and Simon Chisholm, are taking part in the incredible Rag Run dreamed up by a Warrington vodka company.

Students must devise the most incredible, ingenious or daft way of arriving in Warrington on Bank Holiday Monday, May 4.

The vodka makers, Vladivar, have £250 in prize money for the best entries. It will go to the winning colleges' Rag Appeals.

The Bath students are also looking for local sponsors.

The Post Office is sending the students by Datapost, which gives assured delivery. They will travel to London and on to spend Sunday night in Manchester.

Another Bath student entry, which includes the rag chairman, has set off to make its way to Warrington by motorised floating bath tub.

Bath Evening Chronicle report of May 1st 1981

Richard's new GF, Diane, Jeremy and Richard outside the Colton Arms, West Kensington

After a refuel, I had my first bike fall, my mistake. I pushed off from the side stand and it was too heavy for me to hold up whilst slinging my leg up over the saddle. A couple of bemused forecourt attendants gave me a hand to lift her upright; lesson learnt: never try to push off from the side stand whilst dismounted, preferably use the main stand and push off whilst astride.

Dover brought the white cliffs, fish and chips, a last phone call home and then on and up into the iron belly of the roll-on, roll-off ferry to France. Two intrigued lads on a 750cc tourer told me that they were off to Paris; their disbelief was total when I said that I was off to cross Africa.

Farewell to the white cliffs of Blighty

Chapter 4

FRANCE

I**T WAS A CLEAR EVENING, A CALM SEA AND A FINE FAREWELL TO THE WHITE CLIFFS IN** the glow of a setting sun. Calais appeared pretty and the Gothic town hall clock tower drew me to the town's centre where I found a cheap hotel room for the night. Unfortunately, the room was three floors up, so it took about half an hour to detach everything from the bike and carry it all up the stairs to safety. I was dead beat and hit the sack without delay.

A real panic happened on waking the next morning: the bike keys were nowhere to be found. After checking and rechecking through everything I thought I had better see if I had dropped them on the way up. Amazingly, I found them perched on the Suzy's white rear top box where they must have been lying all night. There and then I took a spare tennis shoelace and tied them around my neck and never were they to be placed anywhere else but there for the duration of the trip.

After a quick coffee and most excellent croissants a surprising amount of time was lost in carrying everything back down the three flights of stairs and tying it all safely back on to the bike. Finally, by 11am I was heading out of town on the old RN1. Soon the clouds closed in overhead and it became quite cold riding at 50mph despite my fisherman's yellow PVC over-trousers and jacket.

Not wishing to battle with the traffic heading for Paris I took the bypass for Chartres, after which the rain began in earnest. Several French motorcyclists waved or flashed their headlights as they came towards me in the spirit of a camaraderie of fellow knights of the road.

After a couple of hundred miles I felt very much like stopping but decided to press on for Tours where I knew good food and a hot bath could be waiting for me at my Tante Simone's

Beauvoir – Tante Simone's House at Tours

house above the town. I was so aching, stiff and tired when I arrived in the gathering dusk that I nearly fell again when I tried to dismount. My somewhat startled aunt (who due to signal failure was not expecting me) took pity on me, took me in, fed me superbly and pumped some beautiful red local wine into me from her cellar. I was warm in no time.

Taking full advantage of the comfort and hospitality provided I delayed my departure until after lunch, before which I gave the bike a minor service and check over. Mileage was 642 miles and the spark plugs needed decoking. Then full of ham, cheese and some more of the excellent Sancerre Pinot, I wobbled off on my way once more.

The delightful medieval city of Poitier was the next major town and the sun came out to light up the magnificent limestone edifices of its Gothic cathedral. It remained out all the way to Bordeaux, the best ride conditions to date. However, when crossing the huge bridge over the Gironde entering Bordeaux a strong gust of wind made my rear wheel hop in an alarming way; fortunately I was able to correct the skid, but it was a hairy moment.

In the town's old quarter next to the docks I found a cheap hotel and a cheap and rustic meal was had on the harbourside. Later in my grotty room the mosquitos buzzed me all night and feasted well.

An hour of work in drizzle next morning saw the machine loaded once more. However, I was unable to push off from the bike's main stand as the road camber was far too steep for its release. Stuck, I gestured to a van delivery man opposite; he immediately grasped my predicament and willingly crossed over the road to help me launch.

The weather was terrible for the first hour, fine rain, mist and lots of spray obscured my vision as huge container lorries belted past, some swerving as they too only saw me at the last moment.

Just before reaching Bayonne I clocked up my first 1000 miles slowly climbing up the foothills of the Pyrenees and on to the Spanish border by way of St Jean de Luz.

Chapter 5

SPAIN

I CROSSED INTO SPAIN ON A LONELY WINDING AND REMOTE MOUNTAIN ROAD signed for Pamplona, surprisingly no one to show my passport to, not even a Gendarmes Post. Maybe it was the Basque terrorist war which precluded this. The landscape here was very wild and rugged and from behind every bush by the road I half expected terrorists to jump out brandishing guns and commandeering Suzy after disposing of her foolish rider.

A few kilometres outside of Pamplona I followed a sign away from the road to a campsite. At the end of the track a pair of padlocked gates blocked the entrance and a camper van with a GB sticker was pulled over on a hardstanding. Within ten minutes of arrival I was sitting down to a very unexpected but welcome camper's supper with Bruce and Sheila Parker who hailed from Chipping Norton.

That, my first night in the little two-man green tent, was beyond cold; at dawn I emerged and discovered a layer of ice 10mm thick covering the tent. However, it was a gorgeous sight of the sun rising to a backdrop of resplendent snow-capped peaks that made the night's privations worthwhile.

In Pamplona I found a surprisingly plush bank in which to exchange my unused French francs to Spanish pesetas. I thought to myself, in Spain if anything is doing well after the road building industry, it's the banks.

A quick coffee and then on down the road to the next pretty hill town of Tarazona, passing some more beautiful snow-capped peaks. The labouring engine and reduction of power was very noticeable as we climbed seemingly endlessly further up on to the semi-arid Meseta Plateau and then down through some wild country finally arriving in Madrid at about 7pm in time for their rush hour. I had been planning to try and find a cheap hotel to stay in, but the chaotic state of the capital's roads made me decide it would be a better option to just keep on going despite weariness and find somewhere out in the southern suburbs. I had been hoping to pick up a road map of Madrid from the tourist office but by the time I found it the doors were shut; my general confusion was not aided by a near absence of readable road signs.

It really was not long out of the city centre before I was completely lost in a maze of suburbs full of commuter traffic heading to their homes. Only one thing for it: I put my old trusty Silva compass on top of the map case on my tank bag and headed due south. Often, I have been asked if I ever got lost on my trip and people are taken aback by my reply, "Yes, in Madrid."

Probably by chance I encountered a road signed for Toledo and with great satisfaction carried on south through the steadily decreasing traffic and outlying suburbs as dusk came down. After many more miles I could go no further and spotted a layby in which to make camp for the night. It was not a happy event when in my dismount in total darkness the bike fell over. Everything had to be removed fast as I could smell fuel leaking out of the tank. Then when naked of all the luggage I was, with super human effort, able to lift it upright once more. Too tired to put my tent up, I just jumped into my sleeping bag in the open praying for a clear night. It was a ridiculous day's ride taking twelve hours and some 300 miles. In the morning I discovered that I had lost all my water in the bike fall and only had a small bar of chocolate to breakfast on.

Fortunately, it was only a few kilometres to Toledo where hot coffee and sweet pastries were wolfed down whilst soaking up the ambiance and beauty of the old Royal Capital of Spain. It's one place I have vowed to return to but have not yet achieved. Perhaps I should have stayed a day here, but Africa was calling.

Climbing up away from the town the road finally started to level out onto the vast plains of La Mancha, presenting a barren landscape with few villages and a few whitewashed windmills. Further on were huge vineyards with their vines all cropped back with their first leaves showing.

I stopped for lunch at a trucker's roadside cafe and enjoyed a meal I remember to this day. First a heavy and chunky vegetable soup rich with paprika, followed by a simple plate of grilled chicken on a bed of fried skin-on garlic and finished with a couple of rings of fresh pineapple. Wonderful!

The endless road led on to the end of the plains and to the historic fortress town of Jaen, another town I pledged to revisit in the future.

The narrow road then became more interesting winding up through some really impressive mountains with very steep hairpin bends. In the late afternoon Granada

Mountain Road in Central Southern Spain

appeared with its tremendous backdrop of the snowy Sierra Nevada mountains. I stopped briefly in the town to pick up some supplies during which time the bike was surrounded by a crowd of young student admirers fascinated by her heavy load and surprisingly her compass. Outside the town I found a delightful campsite called Embaise del Cubillas, located by the edge of a cool blue reservoir lake with the snowy peaks clearly reflected in its jewel waters.

Next morning Suzy was not so easy to start with initially only one cylinder firing and the left-hand one spluttering slowly into life as the engine warmed up. I concluded the spark plugs would soon need another decoke and also the points would need a clean, gap check and possibly the timing would need resetting, all jobs I was becoming adept at doing, but that could wait for later.

After a couple of hours' hard riding over the high Sierras I chanced upon a very dry desert-like stretch of country with sand lying on each side. This was Spain's Taberna desert outside of Almeria which has been used to shoot several films and Westerns since the 1950s. Soon the blue Mediterranean came into sight, which was very exhilarating, and I burst into song as we turned right onto the coast road and soon spotted the unmistakable

Farewell Gibralta

outline of Gibraltar in the distant haze. Also in the far distance was the purple outline of the Rif Mountains of Morocco.

Grey skies hung over the ugly industrial port of Algeciras; no sooner was my little green tent up on its poles in the municipal campsite than the first splashes of rain splattered in heavy drops around me. The downpour continued for most of the night; fortunately, early in the evening I had remembered that my boots were still outside. Perhaps my forgetfulness was not aided by the consumption of an entire bottle of ultra-cheap white wine to celebrate my crossing of Europe in just a week, for which my head certainly paid the price the next morning.

Anyway, I was much relieved to discover that my tent, despite lack of flysheet and ridge pole, was truly waterproof; it had been the cheapest I could find in London. This made for very quick erection and dismantling, and the tent incorporated an excellent and later invaluable zipped mosquito net behind the entrance flap and also to its vents.

It was a muddy and wet break-up of camp in the light drizzle of the morning. I followed down to the docks a fellow French biker, on a nice expensive-looking Yamaha 500 Enduro, who was heading to Tangiers from the campsite and who knew where the ferry ticket office was.

After successfully purchasing my ticket and then boarding the ferry I was on the prow deck looking down at the remaining vehicles boarding when a couple of very scraggy, shaggy-haired individuals roared up in a battered Renault 4 and were promptly flagged down and arrested by the Guarda Civil. When the boat left dock fifteen minutes later their car was standing forlornly on its own in the dockside drizzle.

As we sailed out past Gibraltar the sun burst out through the clouds and the view of the rock was truly spectacular. My spirits were further lifted by the splendid sight of two RN destroyers with ensigns fluttering in the harbour across the bay.

Chapter 6

MOROCCO

Ceuta was a fairly attractive Spanish-style town with an abundance of duty-free goods available, ranging from whisky to pocket calculators. A few miles south of the enclave we came across the high wire fence denoting the border with a somewhat Wild West atmosphere of queuing men, women, animals and belongings waiting seemingly all day to get across to Morocco and on the other side an equally large crowd trying to come the other way. The people were sporting brown or stripy coloured and patterned cloaks with pointed hoods as if they were monks from some weird monastery, a massive change in culture; definitely we were in the Third World now.

Not far away from the border I rounded a bend to see an old Renault in the ditch with a dead mule, a grisly reminder of the dangers of the open road and wandering animals, of which I have a few tales to tell – see later!

After Tetouan the road started to climb up into a beautiful Rif mountain; on a remote mountain road Suzy suddenly faltered and then stopped. At first, I thought that it must be the plugs being blocked with carbon preventing a spark, for normally each morning I would remove them and clean them with fine carborundum paper but had omitted to do that on this morning. After dismounting and removing my helmet a strong smell of fuel assailed my nostrils and then I discovered that one of the fuel pipes had disconnected, probably by prolonged vibration, and had sprayed a large amount of fuel which was now puddled on top of the engine casing under the carburettors.

The simple fix was to take some copper wire from my spares and tighten it back on to its spigot with a good nip up from my long-nosed pliers. Soon we were rolling once more with the scenery becoming ever more spectacular. As we passed the little

Fez Municipal Campsite

villages on the way to Fez small boys waved and some playfully threw little stones at me. I figured that it must be the local sport, however I did find the experience somewhat disconcerting.

On reaching the outskirts of Fez a volunteer on a moped guided me through a maze of old medieval streets to the town's municipal campsite. This was built like a fortress with high surrounding walls and lay just beyond the ornate entrance gateway arch through the old city walls. According to the signed campsite regulations no Moroccans were allowed inside the campsite; such a different world, the 1980s. The campsite was like a huge enclosed park with enough space for several hundred tents and caravans. I decided to spend my first proper break here as I had been on the road for more than a week. That night was surprisingly cold, so I pulled my anorak on before wriggling into my sleeping bag for the night.

Next day I gave the bike its first hand-wash and a couple of French bikers came by for a chat and then suggested lunch at a cheap restaurant close by which was good and cheap. Afterwards we went out on a beautiful ride for a few miles across rolling hills carpeted with the first wheatsheaves of spring trying to find the source of the Fez river at a place called Sidi Hazzam, which remained elusive despite several positive directions from various Moroccan field workers.

That evening back at camp I got chatting to a couple of English lads (Mark and Nick) travelling in a battered old Morris Minor Woodie traveller who it turned out had driven all the way from my home town of Bath.

That evening we all decided to drive down to the medina in the traveller and after traversing an endless maze of narrow and twisting streets arrived and parked it close to the very impressive city gateway to the old city, which was adorned with the most exquisite ornamental patterned blue tiles, called the Bab Bou Jeloud.

On foot we strolled through the packed alleyways into the heart of the huge medina, full of character and strange oriental smells. The passages wound in and out, up and down, incredibly narrow in places and even tunnelling through buildings, pitch dark with large ironclad doors behind which one imagined knife-wielding thugs were waiting to burst out and rob young and foolish foreign travellers.

The whole atmosphere was thoroughly medieval with streets full of similar traders huddled together to keep an eye on each other's prices. Now and again little boys would rush up begging for coins or offering to guide you to their uncles' shop, guaranteed to be the best of all in the medina.

Sadly, on other street corners young and not-so-young girls would be squatting with babies on their knees or a young child and all with hands outstretched calling for "baksheesh, baksheesh", the eternal cry of both the Near and Far East.

Others again tried to lure us with, "Master, you must come to my father's shop to buy at special price, you will see he is the cheapest." Others followed us relentlessly from shop to shop insisting on giving a guided tour. Then a passing whisperer would say, "Hashish, you smoke, mister? Follow me."

We stuck close together and were completely absorbed with our surroundings; at length after a glass of freshly pressed orange juice we decided that it was time to leave and go back to the car. We walked for miles around in circles always seeming to return to the same place with not a clue as to where the exit to the medina might be, a complete rabbit warren. We then tried engaging guides who only led us deeper in. After a good two hours we eventually stumbled across another exit gate and decided to take a waiting taxi back to the campsite and from there retrace our route back to the Traveller waiting at the Bab Bou Jeloud. An extraordinary experience I have never since repeated of being so completely lost.

That evening we all squeezed into Mark and Nick's tent; they put on UB40 and rolled a huge joint laced with the local hashish. We were all high in no time at all.

You want Hashish?

In the morning I returned back to the medina on the bike to take some photos, keeping a careful note of my bearings. I took some excellent shots with my little Olympus Trip 35mm camera and met a carpenter who showed me around his workshop and then invited me back to his house for lunch. The women were all in one room and us men in another and we were served a communal lunch which we ate off a single plate using our hands to scope up the rice and vegetables with nobody bothering to wash their hands. Indeed, the only tap for washing of hands feet, etc. was a low-level cold water feed in the small outhouse by the hole in the floor. Cholera, I later found out, has hit Fez on many separate occasions; the Fez river running through the medina has now been concreted over as all the sewerage of hundreds of thousands runs into it, causing horrendous stench and disease.

(Now in 2020 there is a long overdue project underway to open up the river once more to enable clean water to flow down from the mountains and through the town.)

Later that afternoon in the new town I rode up to the magnificent golden door of the royal palace. A guard dressed in a crisp white uniform with a red fez gestured with his rifle for me to go no closer; I decided not to take a photo.

That evening was pleasantly spent with my French biker friends, Michel and Joel, sipping mint tea and discussing my route for tomorrow to head me south and west to the fabled city and old hippy destination of Marrakesh.

By 10.30am I was packed and rolling out of town with no clear signposts, which was a bit of a challenge so I resorted to compass navigation once more and asked directions of as many different people as I could. Usually if you get two answers the same there is a good chance the advice is correct, and three independent affirmations is certainty. Finally, I followed a local on a scooter who had been kind enough to chase me for over a mile after I had taken the wrong turning from his original instructions.

The scenery again was extremely beautiful, starting with gentle rolling hills studded with cedar and pine forests, a smooth tar surface and hardly any traffic. Then we rolled down onto a large fertile plain carpeted with an abundance of different crops. After Kasbah Tadla I reached the crest of a small hill and suddenly was confronted by one of Africa's many splendours: the huge Atlas Mountains displayed themselves towering above with peak after peak capped in snowy glory.

The road then followed the Atlas chain all the way to Marrakesh. Just before reaching the town I passed my first outcrop of rock desert, a little like a red Martian landscape. This caused me to wonder what the Sahara would be like, waiting for me on the other side of this huge range.

Nine hours and 350 miles later I arrived, shattered, exhausted and greatly exhilarated to have made it all the way to Marrakesh. I followed another scooter guide to the municipal campsite outside the old walled town.

By 6.30am the sun was up and it was already too warm to stay inside my tent. I spent the morning exploring Marrakesh on foot. At the tourist office they tried to sell me a tourist map of the town for the equivalent of 50p; however, I declined for it appeared not to be as good as the map I had incorporated in my invaluable guide to Africa written by Geoff Crowther and entitled *Africa on the Cheap*. I found it to be on the whole an excellent guide in spite of the prices and routes being three years out of date. Nearly every overland traveller I was to meet in the next six months had a copy of this masterpiece or else would ask to borrow my copy and avidly take notes about places to stay, visa requirements and local customs, etc. It was a sort of forerunner to the Lonely Planet series of guides produced by a hippy-type commune in London and information fed by an endless stream of travellers' letters which were appended to update each issue's currency. Eventually so many people had fingered this veritable bible it virtually fell apart and had to go onto restricted circulation.

On my morning stroll through Marrakesh I passed through the old red mud city walls and on to another huge medina swarming with pestering touts and would-be merchants.

I tried my hand at haggling for a rather nice tooled leather bag to get the feel of what sort of prices and discount thereon to expect. He started the negotiations quoting forty dirhams, so I offered ten and when he shook his head, I started to walk away. To my surprise I heard, "Oui monsieur, ten dirhams," to which I retracted my offer as I actually did not particularly want that bag. Then as I continued to walk away, I was pursued and to my great surprise the bag was thrust around my neck. I removed it and placed it on a moped parked nearby and continued to walk on. The merchant picked it up again and ran once more after me obviously thinking that I was a more resistant type of tourist than the norm. When he caught up with me, he asked again what price I could offer. When I replied six dirhams he looked as if he was going to spit at me and slowly turned away cursing and muttering to himself.

The main square (Jemaa el-Fnaa) at the entrance to the souk was alive with water sellers and snake charmers who would all stroll up to the lonesome tourist clearly after financial gain so I lied saying it was all old hat to me having been to the city before and then watched them absorbed out of the corner of my eye. One chap hailed me with a snake wrapped

Water sellers at Marrakesh medina

around his headscarf and another with a huge black scorpion stuck on his equally huge Arab nose. "Look master, look – amazing?" I thought to myself that the poor scorpion was so drugged he must have been in danger of falling off but had been glued into fixed position.

In the narrow passages of the medina many beggars sat looking fairly kempt and healthily nourished. But they were hard at work gently touching me on the forearm as I passed by with extended hands and pitiful, pleading eyes, mumbling short passages probably from the Koran. I rarely give money to beggars because of the numerous begging syndicates in existence in the Third World where begging constitutes big business. Children are often sold by their parents to these syndicates because they are too poor to feed them or have too many children already. These children are then put straight out onto the streets to beg. The lucky ones are those who are not deliberately deformed by their new owners. I have seen many instances on an earlier overland trip to India of limbs clearly having been purposely broken and then reset at the craziest of angles to produce the all-important pathetic and helpless appearance. Better than money is the gift of food for these poor people rather than money to go straight into their masters' pockets.

The next evening, I was once more strolling down to the hub of Marrakesh life at the Jemaa el-Fnaa square when I was approached by a boy selling postcards. He had a ten-franc piece which he wanted to trade for a dirham; as this should be worth about eight dirhams I thought that there must be a catch somewhere. Perhaps he wanted to see where my money was kept so I ignored him and passed by none the wiser. I ate a local meal in a tiny shack off the square, which proudly called itself a meat restaurant. The equivalent of just sixty pence bought me a delicious meal of salad, fresh baked flatbread, and two mutton chops grilled over charcoal. The hygiene however was very suspect with grubby plates and various shades of green mould wedged in the corners of the old iron fork with which I was proudly presented after a final finger polish from the waiter. Probably the only one in the place and reserved for the use of special patrons. I decided that my own fingers would be the safest option for eating with and followed the example of my fellow diners, ending with a healthy burp to show my appreciation.

It was on Friday May 15th, exactly two weeks on the road since leaving Bath, and so far with no major problems, when I rode gently out of Marrakesh breezing along a smooth tar highway at a relaxed 45mph climbing up towards the towering and majestic Atlas above. The sky was azure blue, but the mountains were skirted with a light haze. The road sharply increased its incline and the view became more spectacular with each passing mile. Close to the road I passed many small settlements of stone and mud buildings with brightly clothed women scurrying about busily. Small boys by the wayside held out large lumps of coloured rock crystals tempting me to stop and buy.

Climbing up the Atlas

View from the top of the pass

I estimated the highest part of the pass was about 7000ft and Suzy took it in her stride thanks to the very low first and second gearing of her six-speed gearbox. No issue with overheating either despite my removal of the ram air cover cowling to the cylinder head, which had had to be done back in London to enable the fitting of the Bonza fuel tank. In fact, later models of the GT 250 did away with the ram air system altogether.

The south side of the Atlas provided a dramatic contrast to the north side, which had been green, fertile and Mediterranean in appearance. The south side is the boundary of the mighty Sahara and is an arid and desolate place of rock, gravel and sand with a sparse scattering of small oases and few minor towns. The predominant colour is yellow-brown and plants of any type are few and far between.

As I rode down from the mountains the temperature rose dramatically with a new wave of heat hitting me every 500ft or so of decrease in altitude. By the time I had reached the lower foothills I had to halt and strip off my jacket and sweater, which had served me so well in many a cold spot back north. At Ouarzazate, now a world-famous filmmaking location known as Morocco's little Hollywood, but then a dusty, unattractive fuel stop, I lunched, refuelled and calculated by riding at a steady 45 to

50mph I was returning about fifty miles to the gallon, a remarkable saving on 40mpg at 55mph!

Later in the afternoon as I was passing another small oasis town Suzy blew her rear tyre for the first of what was to be dozens of times over the next six months. This surprised me as I had filled both tyres with OVO solution, which claimed to render a tyre after treatment with it to be puncture-proof for life. The sensation of a fully loaded machine having a rear wheel puncture at 50mph is somewhat curious. The machine starts to weave almost drunkenly from side to side then you know you are in trouble when the rear wheel attempts to overtake the front one. Good fortune enabled me to retain balance and control to halt within a couple of yards of the only palm tree for miles around. I pushed the loaded bike into its shade and started to prepare for the repair of my first puncture. Just as I had finished the task of unloading all the gear a young Moroccan and an old man appeared and offered to help me. It turned out that the young man was a mechanic of some sort and he certainly knew how to deal with the tyre. We found that the nipple of the inner tube had completely pulled off, which meant that it was beyond repair. So early in my trip one of my precious stock of four spare inner tubes had to be used. I was puzzled how the puncture had occurred as there were no obvious objects embedded in or evidence of penetration of the tyre. Maybe the blowout was due to a build-up of heat and why did the nipple get pulled off? It was an Avon rubber inner tube of good quality and one of the best on the market.

An hour and a half later the new tube was in, the wheel back on and all my luggage reloaded. A handy stream of water to the side of the road enabled me to wash my hands of dirt, rubber and grease and then we were all invited to a nearby house for tea. Moroccan tea is a delight being made with large green mint leaves stuffed in a glass with lots of sugar over which boiling water is poured.

Our host was a very nice lad, a teacher posted down from Tetouan to the oasis's primary school at El Kelaa. In no time he was working hard attempting to teach me the rudiments of Arabic in between excitedly pointing at the pictures on his wall of Leeds United Football team. After an hour or so in his pleasant company I took my leave as I had to reach Todra Gorge, my target for making camp that night, which I arrived at half an hour after sunset.

Todra Gorge is a very green and fertile oasis by the river, which runs down from the snowy peaks of the Atlas through a Cheddar-like gorge to the settlement. Up the valley there was a most attractive and modern campsite for the few tourists who venture that far. It was surrounded by date palms luxuriant by the light of a rising moon. A stream passed through the centre of the campground and in the moonlight I saw iridescent fish

Up Todra Gorge – as far as I could get

darting in and out of its banks. In the morning I learnt that the reason why these fish are still swimming and not on the dinner tables of the locals was because they had the very good fortune to be sacred and were known as "Les poisons saints aux sources du Todra".

In the morning before leaving the gorge I undertook a challenging rough track on the bike as far as I could ride up the spectacular gorge stopping at my turn point to take a photo.

After Todra the terrain was barren and rock-strewn and a further reduction of speed was forced due to the poor state of the tarmac road surface. It was a curious contrasting sight to be down in the now scorching desert and yet never out of view of the snowy clad peaks left floating as clouds in the sky above.

I reached Kar Es Souk, an old camel train town, by 11am. By then it was too hot to continue the ride, so I parked Suzy under a shady palm tree and stumbled into a café in the town's main street. The local Moroccans were most friendly and soon made me feel welcome in their strange native Berber tongue of which I understood not a word, and alternatively poor French and even some English was attempted. I was invited for lunch by several but was far too exhausted by the approaching midday heat to accept. Many of the patrons were illegally smoking joints despite the presence nearby of the town's two policemen. Law enforcement seemed to be very lax in these parts, perhaps deliberately just to keep the people happy in an old tradition.

In early afternoon I left town and the road narrowed down to a single rough stretch of tar with no other vehicles in sight. Rounding a bend, I saw little yellow humps of sand ahead, my first dunes. At one point one of these dunes had spilled across the tar track and Suzy slewed around in a startling manner nearly causing me to lose control as I optimistically attempted to plough through it at about 30mph, obviously too fast!

A mile further on a much larger dune was completely obliterating the road to a depth of 5ft over a 30ft length. Maybe that was the explanation as to why I had seen not a soul since having left town. This gave me the first opportunity to find out how Suzy would handle in the sand after months of speculation. I drove into the sand cautiously at 10mph and as the rear wheel hit the sand immediately all traction power was lost. I cut the motor whilst straddled astride 3ft deep in the drift and wondered how on earth I would be able to get her out on my own. I pondered for a couple of minutes then the increasing heat from the mid-afternoon sun drove me to action. I discovered by rocking Suzy back and forth on her suspension and then jerking back violently and grabbing the front brake lever at the optimum point I was able to gain an inch or two backwards on each attempt.

After fifteen minutes of extreme exercise in this manner we became free and it took another fifteen minutes for me to recover my breath and strength in the appalling heat.

Road block – the first of several dunes across the highway

As I pondered deep in thought as to how I could further proceed on this route I then noticed 30ft behind me a series of tyre tracks leading off around the back of the dune in an arc of about 50ft. It did not look too promising but there was no other option apparent. I discovered that I was able to make progress on the compressed sand in the middle of a heavy lorry track and slowly progress was made, balance maintained, and the tar track eventually regained to my great relief.

I rode on alone until sunset, skirting around two or three dunes in similar fashion and finally pulled off the deserted highway to camp a hundred yards off the road in no-man's land. This stretch of desert was semi-arid with a few plants and clumps of curiously coloured moss growing on large boulders. I was powerfully overwhelmed by the magnitude and solitude of my surroundings, no other living creature evident possibly for a hundred miles, the only evidence of man being the thin river of tar and an endless line of telegraph poles disappearing into infinity on the horizon. It was a humbling first night in the desert completely alone under a star-studded sky.

Later in the moonlight I began to worry that perhaps I was not completely alone but might have a scorpion encounter. In this part of the world according to my guidebook lives the notorious black scorpion, which I had already encountered on the nose in Marrakesh, whose sting can be very painful and fatal unless an anti-venom is immediately taken. Much to my relief the night terrors subsided and as the wind got up in the night I became concerned about the pegging of my tent and had to re-stake a few of them.

By 9am I arrived at the southern border town of Figuig; I was unsure as to whether I would be allowed to cross the border here to Algeria as no one had been able to advise me on this due to the ongoing Polissaro war over the former Spanish Sahara, so my ride down here had been a bit of a gamble. If denied passage here my plan B was a ride 350 miles back up north towards the Mediterranean coast to cross at Oujda to Tlemcen.

I spent my last dirhams on fuel, food and an irresistible half kilo of butter, which I wrapped in a water-soaked rag and buried in the depths of my food haversack; this worked quite well as long as I kept the rag damp and for the next three days I lived on huge chunks of baguette soaked lavishly in the half molten butter.

Before approaching the border post I hid away my invaluable Michelin map of North Africa in case it might be confiscated due to the war and as decoys placed a couple of tourist office maps of Morocco in my tank bag display holder, which would cause me no pain if they were to be taken. At the border I met a party of German tourists traveling in a pair of VW camper vans; our luck was in and after only half an hour of form-filling a cursory search of luggage was made and as I had thought the decoy maps were confiscated, then we were all waved on in convoy across the 5km stretch of no-man's land to the Algerian post.

Chapter 7

ALGERIA

At the Algerian post we were welcomed with a smart salute from a very colonial-era border post official in a French General de Gaulle-type hat dressed in a crisp blue and gold uniform. It seemed that today was a special day for him as not many travellers passed this way, probably due to lack of information as to whether the post was open or closed for crossing, and today he had a surprise convoy. Compared to the Moroccan border post tents this post was an impressive hotel-style building with air conditioning, courtyards with fountains playing amongst a riot of different exotic plants, and even separate amenities were available for both sexes to shower and go to the loo.

The entry formalities were however lengthy but halfway through the mountain of form-filling the officer suggested that we rest and join him for a stroll around his lovely garden of which he was obviously very proud. By midday after much hand-shaking and "au revoirs" we were on the road once more. The Germans decided to halt for lunch, but I was impatient to press on, so we said farewell with no doubt that we would all meet again as we were taking the same onward route.

The road now ran south-west towards the regional administrative town of Bechar. A strong headwind blew up making it impossible for Suzy to hold power in sixth gear so we battled on at reduced speed in fifth. About half an hour after the wind got up I stopped at the roadside to eat some of my bread and molten butter and within ten minutes no fewer than three trucks stopped to see if I needed help; that put a stop to future picnics so close to the road as it appears to be the code of the desert that you always stop and check out everyone else.

On the far side of Bechar I was pulled up at a police roadblock to check that I was suitably equipped for the long stretch of desert that I was about to embark on. They were very impressed with my large seven-gallon fuel tank and reserve five-gallon speedboat fuel container in my rear top box both brimming with fuel and passed me out as also having adequate stocks of fuel and water. Thirty kilometres further down the road I realised that in fact I needed some Algerian currency, which I should have obtained back in Bechar as my destination of Tamanrasset lay nearly 2000km to the south. I recrossed the police check point much to their amusement and arrived in town to find that the bank had closed. I hammered on the big front doors of the building and the manager kindly agreed as a special favour to an Englishman in need to change some pounds for me. Once more I waved to my police friends as they waved me through their pole barrier for the third time in as many hours.

On my Michelin map I noticed a little tar road branching off to the left towards the vast sea of sand called the Grande Erg Occidental to a little oasis called Taghit. It meant a deviation of some 90km from my route but I was curious to see the famously high dunes located there according to my guidebook. Just after turning off at the junction and stopping to check my map I overbalanced and machine with rider, swiftly sidestepping the falling bike, ended up on the roadside gravel. Leaking petrol heading towards the hot engine was an immediate spur to strip everything off the bike and get the machine back upright, which I achieved in a record five minutes of intense exertion.

About 10km from Taghit I pulled off the road under a sort of rock shelter and pitched camp for the night. As I was exhausted, I just rolled out my sleeping bag under the stars and a spectacularly bright and clear rising moon and tried not to think of scorpions as I drifted off into deep slumber.

What a day for a birthday, my twenty-sixth, all alone and up with the sun. Ten minutes of riding brought into view another of Africa's finest sights. The great dunes of Taghit, which rose impressively to tower a good 500ft above the small oasis seemingly threatening to tumble down and engulf it. Although it was only 9am the sun was already too hot to consider stopping and climbing up these mountains of sand. As it was my birthday, I treated myself to a drink in the luxury hotel at the centre of the oasis. A warm beer set me back the equivalent of £1 but it was well worth it even at that early hour.

Turning around and riding back along the narrow strip of tar towards the main road south I noticed a piste track leading off to my left, which was also marked on my map and appeared to be about 90km long but would save me at least 100km as a shortcut. This would help conserve my fuel as I had no way of being certain as to where the next place to

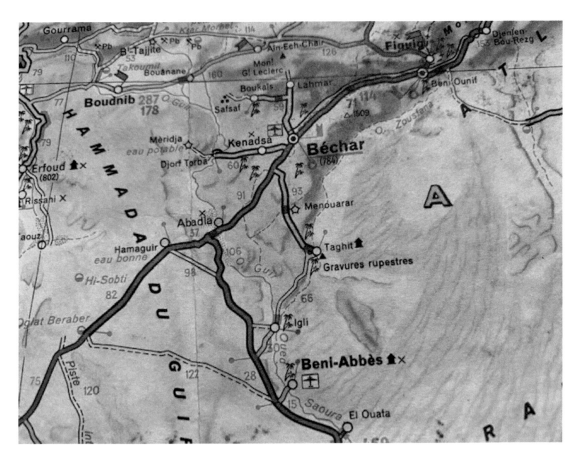

refuel would be. It would also be a good test of Suzy's prowess on groomed desert tracks. Ten kilometres later and after two alarming falls, I knew that this was a foolish decision as should I have an accident the chances of another vehicle passing that day or even later that week would be slim.

Heavily laden Suzy, I started to conclude, would not take kindly to the soft sand grabbing her front wheel unexpectedly. She registered her protest by pulling her front fork legs in a violent twisting manner out of my control inevitably leading to a tumble. Each time we fell I just managed to sidestep off to avert becoming stuck under the machine, then the only way she could be righted by me on my own was to be swiftly stripped of all luggage and then pulled upright. On the last fall she then became bogged down when hauled upright; with the midday sun blistering my helmet I started her and revved furiously and pushed her free. After that second fall, I decided on a final attempt to see if it was wise to continue on this track. I reloaded and purposely rode into the sand once more maintaining my balance; sure enough down dug her rear wheel and the clutch was starting to smell. I placed some stones under the wheel to get some traction and turning

Down but not out!

Time to turn around

around was able to make it back to the narrow strip of tar, then one of her two cylinders went into a misfire. I tried changing a spark plug to no avail. At that point I realised that I would have to head north when back on the highway proper and creep slowly back to Bechar, past my police checkpoint friends once more to sort out this issue and pick up some more fuel.

We crept back along the 90km to town and at the first garage I found I asked if I could use their workshop where I would be out of the beating sun and sheltered from the vicious rasping bite of flying grains of sand. There I spent the whole afternoon trying everything I could think of to cure the misfire; I changed the plugs again, the points, the cylinder head gaskets, but with no success.

Finally, I decided that I must find a bed in town and seek assistance the next day. The only room I could find was in the tourist hotel where I was given a filthy room for $10. What a disappointing birthday it had turned out to be!

"Le petit dejeuner" at the hotel raised my sprits next morning, but my mind was working overtime wrapped up with the health of Suzy. After breakfast I changed the capacitor and cut my finger in the process with my sharp Swiss Army penknife.

I know I would need more time in town so booked a more reasonable and cleaner hotel close by for that night and then set about trying to find a good mechanic. A local on a moped guided me through the streets to an alleged maestro but all he did was check the timing, which I knew to be spot on as I had done that yesterday with my hand timing light. He asked me to return at 3pm to try something else. Not being able to find another mechanic I returned at 3pm to find the door of the shack bolted and strange female murmurings coming from inside. I knocked and called out in vain and could only speculate as to what was going on inside.

At the suggestion of an English-speaking young local I went down to the police station to see if they could be of assistance as they had a fleet of BMWs and presumably a good mechanic to maintain them. They were very courteous, but it soon became evident that they knew all about four-stroke BMWs but not a lot about a two-cylinder two-strokes. This was obvious by the amazed expressions of delight at the painful shriek Suzy emitted when they tweaked her throttle fully open and surprise at the amount of blue smoke blown out of the exhausts as the oil pump injected its maximum rate of two-stroke oil direct into her carburettors. A stupid and pointless thing to do. Eventually they suggested taking me to their own mechanic next morning.

I retired to my new hotel feeling very depressed that evening as all my plans appeared to be crumbling; in need of a shower my mood was not helped by the water being turned off for the afternoon.

This mood was soon lifted by the genuine concern and hospitality shown to me by the new hotel's staff and residents. The manager insisted on Suzy being parked for the night in the restaurant saying jokingly, "Il mange bien".

Next morning Suzy sounded terrible after her rough handling by the police, but at least her wheels were still turning. The police though were as good as their word and led me promptly to their mechanic, Abdullah, who seemed surprisingly competent and professional with his approach. First once more he changed the spark plugs, then he adjusted the synchronisation of the carburettors after which he suspected that the engine was not breathing properly. Sure enough, we then discovered the cause of the problem, so elusive but so simple: both exhaust baffles were blocked with a tarry mix of burnt carbon, dust, sand and oil. They were given a thorough clean and scrub in a petrol bath and larger breath holes were then drilled into the baffles to help the problem from arising again. This was an effective cure as to this day the problem has not recurred although the exhaust noise is a little loud!

I was overcome with joy that Suzy once more was back in good health. The price of three hours' labour asked from by this wizard was only $2, so a substantial tip was definitely in order. That evening I got chatting to a local lad of seventeen who insisted on giving me his brass bangle. I found this embarrassing as I had nothing much to give to him in return. I tried some English money but this was taken as an insult. An hour later he appeared back at my hotel with a flask of special tea prepared by his mother together with a gift of a finely tooled leather pouch made from camel skin. Bechar might not be much of a town but the inhabitants were by and large unspoilt by outside influences, really beautiful people of the desert.

At 4.45am I wheeled Suzy out of the restaurant and rode south out of the town in the haze of a waning moon. By 6am the sun rose and the surrounding desert was getting more arid and hotter by the mile. After covering 200 miles I refuelled at a small oasis by the name of Kerzaz. At the village café the patron made me a couple of cups of lukewarm tea. I was exhausted and a bit gruff with him; when I asked him how much I owed expecting to be rooked I nearly fell off my chair when he replied, "Rien, monsieur," and refused to accept anything.

Foolishly I left this hospitable oasis after only a five-minute rest. Once back on the near molten tarmac I began to regret it as it was after 11am and the heat of the day was reaching its peak. I was also worried about another blowout happening in this arid and shadeless terrain. After half an hour under the merciless sun I found a derelict shelter by the edge of a track, probably used by road construction workers. I lay down for the next five hours on my own absolutely shattered by the intensity of the heat and with fatigue.

Maddeningly, there were too many flies buzzing all my facial orifices to allow for sleep. All I could do to escape their torment was to pull my old army surplus stores mosquito net out of the pack and retreat under its green mesh. This was distinctly uncomfortable as the sweat from my body was running in rivulets and the net soon became as a wet towel. Every so often a fly would perform the seemingly impossible trick of burrowing under the net and buzz around with a maddening drone. Curses of a most venomous nature would erupt from my lips as sitting up I would tear the net away from me and try to evict the intruding invader. The next trick was to lower the net once more over my body without entrapping yet more of the encircling cloud of buzz bombers.

Later after an hour on the road again I was to my great surprise overtaken by a French plated Moto Guzzi. Looking into my rear-view mirror I saw that it was followed by a second one. It was an amazing feeling to have fellow bikers' company again as I had not seen another vehicle of any description for all of the day. We waved crazily to each other before stopping for a chat. At the oasis of Timimoon we were forced to stop by one of the most spectacular sunsets I had yet seen. We then looked for a hotel; the French riders had come all the way down from Calais on a five-week touring holiday. They checked into a couple of rooms and kindly invited me to use their shower and have supper with them. They told me their thermometer had reached 42°C that earlier day. We had a superb French-style meal washed down with ice cold beer and just before midnight I took my leave and set out into the desert to sleep free of charge in a room without walls and more beautiful than any building could provide. I had been exactly three weeks now on the road.

Before sunrise we were moving again north-north-east, bound for El Golea and the junction with the N1, the only tarred road south to the middle of the Sahara where it terminates at Tamanrasset.

In a weak and hazy dawn, a fierce headwind blew up whipping streamers of flying sand and dust. The strength of the breeze caused Suzy to struggle even in fifth gear. The sand cut into my face despite my full-face helmet visor and also into my unprotected ankles like a thousand hot needles as we plunged through cloud after cloud of this abrasive mix. As a truck rolled by in the opposite direction a pebble flew into my cheek causing my face to ache but not breaking skin. The desert now became a mix of dunes, stones and rocks with very little in the way of vegetation. To my relief after an hour and a half the wind died down as I joined the start of the main trans-Saharan route from El Golia to In Salah.

El Golia was sixty-three kilometres to the north but I needed to go there for more supplies of food and fuel. The road was blocked in several places by encroaching sand dunes of various sizes. I now had the experience to know that for me, apart from the

A hazard clearly explained

Or not!

smallest ones which I could plough over in the tracks made by other vehicles, there was no way across them and I had to search for the best route around each one. Once more turning off the road to join a circumnavigating track, Suzy tumbled over and all was panic for five minutes whilst I stripped her down and pulled her upright once more.

The heat was beginning to build up inside my white helmet and it was a relief that we passed the 20km sign to our goal. This was short-lived as all at once one of the cylinders cut out; this was unusual in mid cruise and on inspection I discovered a trace slick of sticky oil residue oozing from the left-hand cylinder head. I decided in view of the rising heat to carry on the journey to El Golia with the greatly reduced power of a single cylinder to find shade before tackling the necessary repair work.

Years before I recalled having had a similar problem on a journey in snow and had resorted to a single cylinder completion of the trip with no other issues arising.

As we limped into El Golia thirty minutes later I was very impressed with Suzy's stamina and celebrated by buying a cold lemonade and, wonder of wonders, an ice cream! That afternoon I took off the left pot cylinder head and reversed the aluminium gasket to see if it would seal better in an inverted position rather than dip into one of my dwindling supplies of spare gaskets. That seemed to do the trick and just as I was completing my repairs an Italian called Tony came over and introduced himself.

It seemed that he was a merchant seaman on leave, a rather shady character I thought. His torso was covered with scars and tattoos denoting to me a violent past. He was travelling in a Lancia and had driven some 800km from Algiers in a day. He appeared to be terrified of the desert and seemed to have no idea of where he was going; I was the only traveller he had stopped to meet so he was rather latching on to me. When he heard that I was intending to leave that evening as soon as it was cool enough, he said, "Let's crossa de desert together," then, "Letsa go to Kenya or any damn place together. This placea no good. Italy no good. I wanta finda some money." Hardly the company I would have chosen but clearly dangerous to offend so reluctantly I set off with him. Having ridden the first 100km with no incident it was by then pitch dark and I was bouncing in and out of potholes and dodging around dunes too big to ride through. Tony's Lancia was hardly built for running on sand and he let out a loud wail of anguish "Mama Mia" when his low-slung machine ground to a halt, front wheels churning furiously ever deeper into the sand. Fortunately a truck came by a few minutes later and with the aid of a steel cable hauled the protesting Lancia out backwards for Tony to try another route around the dune.

Back on the tar strip a few minutes later it was my turn for drama: Suzy hit one pothole too many and the rear tyre blew out. Tony pulled up behind and asked, "Whata da matter?"

"A puncture," I replied.

"What dat?"

"Kaput," I said, pointing to the flat tyre illuminated in the Lancia's headlights.

"Jesus Christ, now what to do?"

"No problem, I can repair," I replied.

But Tony like all rats of his nature was pretty frightened when the chips were down and it was all I could do to persuade him to stay whilst I repaired the puncture by the light of his car, a full two-hour job. During this job Tony told me that he could never return to Italy but did not elaborate as to why. It was left to me to speculate as to whether he was wanted for murder, or by the Mafia or in trouble with his wife!

Sadly, the puncture repair only lasted 10km, the repair patch blew off and this time the outer tyre ran right over the inner tube tearing the inflation nipple right off the tube. Again fortunately this occurred only ten paces from a Range Rover in trouble with five Arabs aboard. Their differential had locked up and they feared to go on in case of further damage to the transmission, so they were stranded for the night waiting on a mechanic next day. Tony left me some cigarettes and then to my relief disappeared into the night. The desert was dangerous enough, I felt, without the company of a madman. The Arabs pulled their Range Rover off the road and helped me get Suzy off it as well for fear of obstructing any trucks coming in the night. We all then bedded down for the night, me in my sleeping bag by my bike and them by the side of their vehicle.

An hour before the dawn I started struggling to get the rear wheel detached and then once more removed the outer tyre casing with my small set of three tyre spanners. The rim belt which covers the top ends of the spokes had disintegrated and would be of no further use; fortunately I had a replacement in my spares, however a new tube was also needed and I only had two left of my original stock of four. If nipples continued to rip off with every other puncture I was going to end up in deep trouble.

As I cruised along at 50mph weaving in and out of the more noticeable potholes I passed a sign for In Salah 290 kms away. With the sun rising ever higher overhead the ride became akin to sitting across a sausage in a frying pan. It was close on midday and far too late to be riding when we rolled into In Salah. Waves of heat exhaustion hit me as I stopped the machine in the merciful shade cast by a date palm down a sandy side street. Strange to say Suzy took to the heat overall extremely well; before leaving home I had suffered all sorts of debates with myself as to whether she would overheat in spite of being air-cooled, but as it turned out her engine lapped up the hot air whirring as a giant fan.

At In Salah there was only one hotel with a dirty room available for £7 with a shared cold shower and a bonus of ice cream just next door – whoopee!

In Salah was left behind in the faint light before dawn and the road surface deteriorated significantly with many more potholes and missing edges than before, but there were no sand dunes as the nature of the terrain had changed to gravel and rock. At 10am just before it was becoming too hot to comfortably ride I arrived at a small nomad encampment by the name of Arak, a distance of 274km (171 miles), not bad going.

I parked Suzy in the meagre shade of a hut made from packing cases and was greeted with "Salaam Alaikum" ("Peace be on you"), the two words the entire Arab world resonates to. Automatically my cracked lips responded "Alaikum Salaam" ("And unto you peace") and an old man of the desert, his eyes flashing as a hawk's, his face swathed by a Jellabiya, stretched his hand to me. I was given tea and a cigarette and boy, what tea it was. The Tuareg call it their whisky, it is like a grey gunpowder in appearance and so strong and sweet you can feel it coursing your veins as you drink it. The glasses are small, but tradition dictates that it should be refilled three times to all around. To do less than that would be to give offence. After this ceremony I presented the old chap with an orange, which he accepted with some delight as nothing grows at Arak. They were intrigued by me setting up my little petrol stove and my brewing up of "English Tea" for all by courtesy of Lipton's teabags!

The stove was greatly admired but the tea must have been like drinking hot sweet water to them and they expressed to me great sorrow that poor white people only had this insipid brew to drink.

Later one of the Tuareg lads led me over to his "bar" as he called it. A metal box hut with a door at each end to allow for any puffs of breeze which might blow up to flow through the hut and cool the interior. There we chatted mostly in sign language and pidgin French then dozed waiting for the heat of the day (45°C plus) to dissipate.

Towards sunset I took Suzy with remarkably an extra passenger of the Tuareg lad on board up the spectacular gorge of Arak to the petrol station at the top. Fortunately, as I was running low, there was some fuel in stock, but it was low octane grade, the pump was broken and the petrol had to be hand cranked, which was a lengthy procedure. I had to wait about an hour and a half for my turn to be fuelled as a couple of trucks had got there before me. There was also an Italian couple who arrived heading north in an old battered Land Rover. They had come up all the way from Burundi and were very kind to me and fed me some soup. After they left I felt exhausted from the heat of the day and went off to crash out early once more away in the desert under the stars.

I left Arak at 4am to tackle the remaining 390km to Tamanrasset; in the dark the very frequent potholes were dangerous and the further we went the worse the road became. The tar was so eroded that for the last 150km most traffic gave it up as a poor job and just drove on either side of it on the desert surface. Apparently, the route was only laid to tar six years before, a classic example of how badly prepared roads can cause a ruined surface. Particularly under conditions where temperatures can range from freezing to more than 45°C. As the road was so bad, I could only average a speed of about 20mph as a result of which I arrived later than planned at the dangerously uncomfortable hour of high noon.

In the town the first foreigner I encountered was my old companion Tony with his green Lancia; he had now decided to go back up north and was about to start his return so swiftly I took my leave of him.

The streets of Tamanrasset were wide and shady, and the town was almost pleasantly cool being at an elevation of over a mile in the sky. Soon I found a café, parked up and stumbled inside for tea, the most refreshing of drinks in a hot climate. Later as I looked for some cheap lodgings I came across a couple of Easy Riders from America on tiny Honda 50s which they had bought and ridden down from Morocco. They were true to type both with Stetsons, Southern drawl and most amusing. Their pleasant plans were to leave the mopeds in Tamanrasset and fly up to Marseilles where they wanted to buy a Peugeot and drive it back down and across the Sahara to sell it and make a fortune in Benin. They had been sparked into this idea by a number of other entrepreneurs doing this and all heading to Benin where the best on sale prices were then to be had. As it turned out nearly every other Westerner I met in Tamanrasset was heading with both cars and trucks down this way to trade in West Africa. I even met a truck with a nearly brand-new car in the back. Clearly there was money to be made.

Later on, back in the café I looked up as two of the party of Germans I had crossed the Algerian border with strolled in. They were pleased to see me and were good company for the afternoon; that morning I lost my water bottle on the road and they immediately offered me one of theirs as a replacement. I got a real buzz from the sense of camaraderie, shared hospitality and overall generosity of fellow overlanders that I had the good fortune to meet.

Having asked around I found out that the best place to camp was 20km north of Tamanrasset at a place called "The Source" where there was a fresh spring of mineral water. The water in Tamanrasset was not very palatable and, with only two public wells in town, difficult to obtain. The desert track leading to the Source was pretty rough going, in places I crawled along in second gear at about 10mph feet outstretched on either side to avoid overbalancing in the sand tracks and to enable a hasty righting kick should it be required. At the Source I discovered a few fellow travellers camping with tents etc. centred on a mud-built house which had been constructed right on top of the spring, which served as a small restaurant for the campers.

The first thing I did after a massive drink was to fill my twenty-litre water container with beautiful clear cool water from the spring pool, then I descended into the valley below for a glorious shower achieved by hanging the container from a tree branch and turning the tap on.

As I climbed back up to camp, much refreshed after my first wash in days, I met a Japanese guy who introduced himself as Kutz as he crawled out of his igloo-style tent. We took to each other immediately although his English was very poor and his French non-existent. It happened also that he was travelling through Africa on a motorcycle but in the reverse direction to me. He had shipped his Yamaha XT 500 scrambler from Japan to Mombasa and was on his way to tour Europe. He had covered many of the roads which were to take me from the West to the East of Africa and had many tales to tell of his travels to date. Most scary for him was the time he broke down in a game reserve in Zaire. He claimed that he was surrounded by roaring lions as he lay quivering in his igloo. I was most impressed as to how he had managed so bravely to travel through some of the most troubled countries in the world speaking no other language but Japanese and very little English, quite remarkable.

English might be the most common international language of the world but in West Africa it might as well be double Dutch; French is the only common Western language in use thereabouts.

Next day, Kutz and I decided to tour the Hoggar area together and to try to visit the Hermitage at Assekrem so in the morning we rode back down the road to Tamanrasset to get fuel and supplies for this trip. In the town I bumped into the first English travellers who were on a Tracks overland expedition travelling in a large pink ex-military Bedford lorry. Their travel companions were a mix of Australians, Germans, Dutch and Swiss and were all very friendly.

As Kutz and I were taking tea at a café a couple of riders came from the south out of the desert and collapsed, dust bedraggled and exhausted, on two chairs opposite us. I dived for my polythene bag of source water and only after they had slaked their thirst were, they able to tell their story. Three months previously they had shipped their big XT 500s to Dakar on the Ivory Coast and were riding the reverse route of the now famous Paris–Dakar Rally back to Paris. This annual event was organised by BMW and has a great following amongst the French. Three of them had left Agadez in Niger five days before and all had gone well until they reached the Algerian border at In Guezzam, a small oasis with a few bamboo huts and an occasional supply of fuel. One hundred and fifty kilometres north of the border, one of their party, blinded by dust as a heavy truck passed by, rode straight into a large rock. His machine survived but he suffered a fractured pelvis

Just out of the desert – Dakar to Paris

My water, fresh from the Source

and was unable to move. One of the pair stayed with him whilst the other raced back to the border to try to arrange a rescue operation. Usually there is a doctor and sometimes a chopper on call at In Guezzam but not that day. Eventually he found a Land Rover and guided it back out next day to the scene of the accident. They all then returned back to In Guezzam and then struggled to arrange a medivac flight up to Tamanrasset and from there on to Paris but unfortunately this also had not been possible. So the next day the Land Rover set out on the two-day journey across the desert once more and back up to Tamanrasset with the injured man in the back. Five days later they gave us the happy news that their friend was safe and under medical care in Paris.

Hearing this tale and knowing Suzy's behaviour in off-road conditions made me realise that it would be foolhardy in the extreme to consider riding across the remaining 800km of desert from here to Agadez with no made-up road, alone and unaided. So, I decided that the best plan would be to find a truck heading south and see if I could buy a ride across.

That afternoon back at the Source I lightened my load by shedding some non-essential items and then departed with Kutz for our run up to Assekrem. The views from the piste were very beautiful and the groomed surface reasonably good. As we climbed up into the Hoggar we left the sand behind and ran over ancient volcanic rock and lava. Just before Assekrem the road rose extremely steeply so that Suzy even in first gear could not climb up. I dismounted and walked her up using 5000 revs and half riding her on the clutch going up in a zigzag fashion. Five hundred foot below the mountain's summit was the Hermitage, just a stone shack before the top of a curiously shaped volcanic peak appearing as a Japanese temple-style painting. There was a small parking and camping area surrounded by a low stone wall and as we arrived the sun had begun to set. We leapt off our machines and rushed to climb the remaining 500ft to just catch the sundown.

Before dawn we were both up and hiked once more up to the top of the peak to catch the first rays of the new rising sun. At 2198m we were panting for breath when we got there.

In the stone chapel, Mass was to be celebrated by the small community of hermits and we were welcomed in to share the service. A dim candlelit passage led from a low timber-framed door into a rush matted room with an altar. In an adjacent room was a small library of early French manuals about the Hoggar region and the Sahara. It was a simple Mass said in the French vernacular conducted by one of the pair of hermits in residence attended by us, a couple of other travellers and a couple of nuns. Afterwards all were invited by the nuns to take coffee. One of the nuns said that she had lived here for thirty years and the hermit Father with impressive flowing beard had been there for twenty-six years. It must be an extraordinary life for them so cut off from the rest of the world but for the odd traveller such as ourselves passing by and the occasional nomadic Tuareg.

On the track back to the Source, Suzy clocked her first 5000 miles of the trip.

Back in Tamanrasset next day I managed to find a truck driver who was prepared to take me across the next 800km stretch of desert to Agadez. His truck was a fairly well beaten up old Berliet with, I noticed, cracked tyres. He told me that he had made the trip many times and as he seemed to be a nice fellow, I decided to chance it. I had had zero luck in finding a lift elsewhere. We arranged to meet, to my frustration, a couple of days later at the customs post south of the town.

The Hoggar tour

View from the Hermitage at sunset

Kutz on his Honda

That afternoon as I tried to take a rest under a shady palm in town a small dust storm bore down and in no time at all I was covered head to toe with dust and every orifice as well. The solution, not too comfortable due to the heat, was to climb into my sleeping bag and pull my head in under its cover. I rode this out for a good couple of hours until the storm passed. Later I went to the bakery to stock up on bread for the next part of the journey as the next day, Friday, all of what shops existed would be shut. After a four-hour enforced wait I secured a couple of loafs; shopping in Tamanrasset was very frustrating as few commodities were available. The baker was a horrible old man and being the only one in town wielded his power mercilessly. That afternoon he had a small argument with one of the customers and so he took it out on everyone else by shutting up shop for a couple of hours leaving about a hundred people outside waiting for bread whilst he simmered down. This meant that it was pitch dark by the time it came for me to ride back up the hairy track into the mountains to the Source. It took me a good hour to cover the 25km back, fortunately with no falls.

Outside to the south of Tamanrasset there is a square just beyond the filling station where the customs clearing station is situated. Surrounding the customs hut was a motley collection of twenty or more vehicles which had been impounded. Here I was to meet the ancient Berliet at 8am.

An hour late the yellow monster drove into sight, groaning loudly with bulging sides and piled high with mountains of sacks of dried dates. It was with some misgivings that I wondered how on earth they would find room for both me and the bike but Musman, the French-speaking Tuareg truck driver, assured me that there would be no problem. The machine would though have to lie sideways atop the date sacks. This would necessitate the draining of the bonza fuel tank which I had just completely filled. Before I started to do this, I passed my luggage up to the truck top load and then to my surprise Musman asked me to ride the bike for a few kilometres prior to loading her up on top as well. He tried to explain the reason for this to me in his bad French which I took to mean that as customs had just cleared him he wanted to take off as quickly as possible and feared that if they spotted the bike on board there might be problems for him. I tried to argue with him but realised very quickly that it was a lost cause and that I had better play along with him.

The first 25km was a breeze anyway on a crisp newly tarred surface; on this stretch we completed the tricky manoeuvre of transferring my helmet from the lorry cab to my head without stopping as the sun had started to beat powerfully down.

After 20km we reached a section where the road was under construction by the Algerian Army. The truck turned off onto a gravel piste alongside, but the surface was so bad I decided to stay on the new tar to keep up with the truck. As I approached a group of

Ignore this at your peril

soldier workers, an officer held up his hand for me to stop. I knew that he would ask for my papers etc. which were, along with everything else of mine, on the truck. To explain this was beyond my French capabilities. Just as I was level with him, I made as if to stop, I then opened my throttle and roared away from him to the amazement of him and his sappers who quickly grabbed lumps of rock and threw them after me just missing my left leg.

The going began to get much more difficult with numerous potholes and boggy sand patches on a very rough surface. I signalled to Musman to stop so that we could now load Suzy aboard. I attached a length of window sash cord, which I had brought with me from home as a transport contingency, to Suzy's front fork hoping that it would withhold the strain of some 145kg. To my horror I realised that all the combined strength of four of us could do was to lift her some 3ft off the ground and no further. Lifting her 12 ft to rest on top of the load was completely unattainable.

Our efforts had not been helped by the presence of the fourth member of the lifting party, a fat Arab who really just pretended to help and later I discovered that he was the owner of the truck and did nothing much other than sit and squeeze his fat fingers incessantly. This vehicle was currently so overloaded that even on the better stretches of piste it could not do more than 40km per hour.

With a sinking feeling in my stomach I had now to acknowledge the inevitable, that I would have to ride through this most notoriously difficult stretch of desert after all. I calculated that I had probably just enough fuel to make In Guezzam on the Algerian border approximately 350km away where I might be able to source some more if I was in luck. Also, maybe we could there find extra hands to help load the bike.

A few minutes after setting off once more we were overtaken by the most surprising sight of a brand new 2.5l Rover saloon with a big strapping man at the wheel, wife beside him and two daughters behind, all as if they were out for a Sunday afternoon drive were it not for the four suitcases strapped to the roof rack.

There is meant to be some control on the suitability of vehicles crossing this stretch of the Sahara, for obvious reasons. I had to get an official permission slip to leave Tamanrasset from the town hall as well as satisfy various roadblock checks. Theoretically it was also a condition that no vehicle is allowed to proceed unless in a convoy of at least two others. Musman must have had some influence in order to escape from this irksome regulation, but this man was completely blissfully unaware of any of these controls and nobody had objected to his outing or if so a couple of dollars no doubt assisted their passage.

When I encountered him later in the day, he was indeed a worried man. "Never again," he kept muttering many times over in the next few days. Errol and Jaqueline came from Surinam and had just spent a month on holiday in Europe.

In Holland he had purchased the car tax free and had heard that it was possible to drive across the Sahara but had obviously done not a lot of research. Seeing a red line on the map going across the desert had boosted a false confidence such that he, a quantity surveyor, was going to drive all the way back to Sokoto, Nigeria where he was working for Roads Nigeria Ltd. Errol was a giant of a man with a very straight and practical approach to life; woe betide anyone who crossed swords with him for he admitted that he had a quick temper. We got on well together and I probably owe him one of my lives!

Anyway, he was very relieved to have joined up with us and after offering liberal quantities of cigarettes to Musman, we all agreed to stay together and off we all set once more.

By the time the heat of the day was reaching its peak and my lips were getting badly cracked with the dryness of the air we had covered about 150km through the sand and gravel, and unloaded, the bike was pretty good fun to ride, and I was encouraged and confident that I could possibly make it across. The tracks on the desert surface across this area were numerous and widely spread out as far as one could see all heading north or south, so our convoy spread out too with some distance between us. Occasionally the bare skeleton of long abandoned vehicle would appear picked clean of anything removable to the very last nut and bolt by the Tuareg and left for the sand to scour off the paintwork.

The lorry halted, I hoped for a rest from the scorching sun and a bite of lunch, but when I approached, I could see they were in trouble; the battery tray had fallen off its ancient mountings. Milwaukie, the lorry's resident mechanic, took some hemp rope which had been holding down sacks of dates and used it to tie the tray back onto the truck. A good repair which lasted the next four days.

On and on we went, the lorry in front and then sometimes behind me, to my left or to my right though never more than half a mile away, each making our own tracks across the hot desert surface. At other places all three vehicles closed up and it was during such a close formation that we hit our first patch of really deep soft sand. I was in the lead when without warning Suzy went out of control zigzagging along as I kept the power up for fear of coming to a halt and getting stuck and transferred my balance from side to side to keep upright. As she was unloaded, she tended to float rather than sink in the thick sand as long as sufficient speed was maintained – a challenge but again good fun – however, her choice of direction was rather like a bolting horse. Previously I had also let some air pressure out of the tyres to improve traction.

The ground clearance for Errol's Rover was not particularly high and Errol although driving at speed came to rest halfway across a 30m sandy stretch. The Berliet ploughed through a full 25m before it too became completely bogged.

This was to be the first bogging down of many during the next few days. The freeing procedure for the lorry was to scrape away the sand by hand around the truck wheels (no shovel was apparent on board!) then a pair of very bent and battered sand ladders were laid down under the leading edge of each rear tyre and then with all pushing from the rear the drive was engaged and progress made. This operation was repeated three times before firmer ground was found.

Carrying the ladders, two men to each for they were fabricated from sheet steel and very heavy, we walked the few metres back to Errol's car who had on his own been trying to dig out his car. Without these ladders Errol's Rover would have been added to the thousands of other abandoned vehicles strewing the whole route across the desert.

Using these 12ft ladders it was a fairly easy job for us to prise the car out of the sand; Musman also suggested reducing the car tyre pressure by three-fifths, which then worked well for the Rover as it had done for the bike.

Approximately 200km out of Tamanrasset and at about 2.30pm, I suddenly felt the by now all too familiar symptoms of a rear tyre blowout. As I came to a halt, I glanced down to confirm my suspicions and then looking up saw with horror the lorry continuing on and then disappearing from my view over a low rise in the gravel half a mile ahead. Very fortunately Errol was not far behind me and when he saw that I was in trouble he charged off to stop the lorry and inform them of my predicament.

There I was broken down and on my own in the desert with no water, tools, or anything much else miles from anywhere in the world's greatest desert. It was eerily quiet and lonesome with no defining feature in view. After what seemed like an age, but probably was only about ten minutes, I heard Errol returning with the truck. It was only two weeks later whilst staying with Errol and Jaqueline in Sokoto that he told me about the delay in returning with the truck to my aid. The fat Arab owner of the truck had at first forbidden Musman to return for me and it was only Errol's aggressive response and a threat to his well-being that had changed his mind. All he was interested in was getting his heavy load of dates to market in Niger with the minimum of delay. I was a nice extra bonus $50 cargo for him as long as I did not cause inconvenience.

On his way back to me Errol spotted a low mound of gravel almost as if it had been placed there for the very purpose of making a ramp; this was a good piece of luck as we had not seen any other mounds similar so far on the journey. It was situated about half a

A skeleton

And more!

Bike now loaded – Milwaukie in foreground

mile away; slowly, I rode Suzy across the sand with her flat tyre and up to the top of the mound. The lorry pulled up alongside and using one of the sand ladders as a ramp we were able with little difficulty to haul Suzy up onto the top of the date sacks where she was then carefully laid on her side.

I soon discovered that being atop the Berliet was like being on some fantastic ship of the desert, slowly weaving its way over the most desolate of the world's oceans. The views were tremendous and the rocking sensation fairly gentle as we wallowed from one sandy drift to the next.

Every once in a while, either the truck or the Rover would get stuck in the sand and then it was all hands to the manning of the ladders and digging, which was quiet exhausting work even in the relative cool of the late afternoon. An hour after dark Musman called a much-needed halt and within two minutes of stopping a fire was lit and a blackened pot of tea put on for the boil. After three cups each of the ritual "whisky" had been imbibed another fire was set in a scooped-out sand hollow; a sack of wheat flour was produced, and some dough was mixed up. As the fire burnt down to form embers they were covered with sand and the roll of dough in a patty shape was placed on top. After ten minutes of baking it was turned over and then buried in more sand for another ten minutes after which it was pulled out of the sand oven and the crust and sand pulled off leaving a kind of unleavened bread.

During this time on the other fire a large metal cauldron was placed containing chopped up camel meat, onions, carrots and tomato paste. After boiling for about thirty minutes it would be poured over the broken-up bread into a large metal bowl. We all sat around in a circle and were invited to dip our right hand into the stew and gorge ourselves. One of the greatest insults in the Arab world would be to use a left hand in a communal bowl, for that is unclean and to be used for personal hygiene. The punishment for theft in some interpretations of the Koran is amputation of the right hand, hence a thief can never again be able to eat communally or to shake hands. Also, it is believed by some that they take this shame with them to the afterlife.

The lumps of camel meat turned out to be pretty tough but quite like beef in flavour; it certainly exercised the jaw bones. That night we all slept on the ground together under the stars, which hung like jewels in the dark sapphire firmament. For the very first time on this trip I spied the Southern Cross low on the horizon, which left me awestruck at the beauty and magnitude of the universe above and our small insignificant existence below.

Well before dawn we were once more rolling again, Musman seemingly certain of the correct direction to navigate like the desert nomad he was; he managed to read the tracks so that we did not get stuck again until the early afternoon as we approached In Guezzam and the Border with Niger.

Nothing but sand

Camel train behind in the distance

In this area the conditions deteriorated severely and all vehicles passing had to be laboriously dug out or left abandoned, more frequent than milestones. This time the Berliet got stuck so deeply that the sand covered the axles and a massive excavation entailed to enable the sand ladders to be inserted under. Finally, after much digging undermining virtually the entire lorry and Milwaukie scurrying around tirelessly like some desert rat, the ladders were squeezed under and bent crazily as the full weight of the twenty-ton lorry and load cut into them. The truck struggled free peeling off long strips of rubber from the cracked tyres of its eight rear wheels. The whole operation took us an hour and a half. In celebration another tea ceremony was indulged as reward for our efforts whilst the fat master sat in the shade of the truck having done absolutely nothing to help.

Later in the afternoon we came across some curiously shaped rocks with sheltered clefts hewn over eons of desert winds, sun and rasping sand. A strange smell of decay wafted up as we prepared to eat. Glancing around I saw the camel meat once more being unwrapped from its rag anti-fly covering and it appeared now to be green in colour and had a life of its own as it was crawling with maggots. The worst-invaded parts were cut off with my ever popular sharp penknife and the less bad parts of the leg were then placed over the fire flames and then struck sharply with a stick producing a small shower of tumbling maggots, the remaining good meat was then chopped up and thrown into the stewpot.

I should mention that by this stage of the trip I was getting used to all manner of hardships. One of many examples was the lorry's water supply; it was held in a recently emptied gasoil drum which it seemed that nobody had bothered to clean out before filling it with well water. Now and again the goatskin slung over the side of the wagon would be topped up from the polluted drum and the outer surface of the skin was moistened by pouring a couple of cupfuls of water over it to cool it to produce tepid water rather than boiling, by the power of evaporation. The water drawn out of the goatskin for drinking would not only taste strongly of diesel oil but would also be opaque in colour with foreign particles floating in it such as goat hairs, brown blobs and little moving organisms, both of undetermined nature.

By the second day I became used to it and seemed to be immune from any damage to my health from its impurities; I even took to enjoying my oil-flavoured hot water of which several litres a day were required particularly after a heavy lorry digging-out session.

Just before sunset we came to a cluster of huts surrounded by some parched and scorched vegetation, which turned out to be In Guezzam. The going was meant to be improved from here to Arlit where a new tarmac road leads from the uranium mines down to Agadez. However, Musman for undisclosed reasons best known to his boss chose to drive along the old route to Agadez, which passed some distance west of Arlit, so Errol and his family left us with a fond farewell and teamed up with another couple of cars going via the newer and better route.

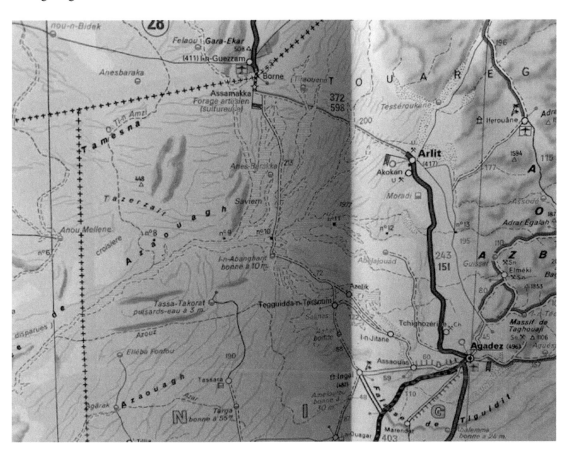

Chapter 8

NIGER

THE ALGERIAN CUSTOMS POST WAS WELL KNOWN FOR SENDING PEOPLE BACK across the desert to Tamanrasset if they were not satisfied that their documents, clearances and permissions were not in order. Thus it was with some trepidation that I entered the customs hut as all was not in order with my declarations due to a black market currency trade I had undertaken a few days before in Tamanrasset. As one enters and exits many African countries use a currency declaration form. On this form is recorded all forms of currency the traveller has including bank notes and travellers' cheques etc. This is to ensure that the Government can legally "rip off" the traveller as he or she is under legal obligation that all currency exchanged is done at an authorised exchange bank or agent at punitive rate. This ensures that the cost of money for the traveller will be on a par with European prices or greater. This legalised theft is particularly offensive in some countries, the set official rates sometimes being as high as twenty times the black market rate therefore the black market was widely used and available but with obvious risk for most travellers.

In Tamanrasset I had exchanged $10 with an overland group who had too many dinars left, but my problem was that I had declared only $70 on my currency form and had about $100 undeclared all in $20 bills. By exchanging only $10 I was in trouble for I would have either too few or too many dollars, according to my form. I decided that the best ploy would be to over-declare rather than under-declare the dollars as they would otherwise be bound to suspect a black-market deal. The other surplus dollars were well hidden inside my roll of toilet paper. It would be no good saying that your money had been stolen or lost, they would probably send you all the way back to Tamanrasset to get a police report as evidence for the theft. Inside the customs post, sure enough, I was asked to show my passport, currency declaration form, medical inoculation certificates, carnet de passage for the bike, etc. and then suffered the indignity of being asked to produce all of my declared money for counting. Slowly the customs officer flicked through my traveller's cheques and then my sterling bank notes before the dollar bills. After a careful recount he said, "Monsieur you have eighty dollars, not seventy dollars." I registered complete surprise and smiling with delight asked him to check again and as I was still beaming as if overcome by the good news of possessing $10 extra than I had thought, he handed me back my money saying, "Lucky for you it was not the other way around"!

As soon as we had cleared customs and the truck had been refuelled, Musman headed us south again into the gathering gloom of the approaching night and after a hundred yards or so we were once more stuck in sand, so back to digging and manoeuvring with the sand ladders again. Then on to help another truck in a similar predicament after which we were shouted at by the border guards to clear off as vehicles were not supposed to halt in no-man's land between the border posts. We carried on until we were out of their sight and then Musman called a halt for the night whilst we remained in no-man's land. The camel stew was particularly strong in flavour that night!

After dawn we arrived at the Niger border post at Assamaka. There we were met with a wonderous sight of a pipe sticking out of the sand with a U-bend sending a steady stream of silver bore water down into a concrete trough below. What a joy it was to put one's head underneath and totally immerse one's body, clothes and all, to its cool massage. It smelt sulphurous, as of rotten eggs, but at least it was cool, clean and fresh.

At this custom post I was asked to lay out the contents of my backpack and other bags for inspection. This went off with no problems and after about an hour we were all allowed to continue our journey. Just half an hour later we were once more stuck but this time in sand of three inches depth lying over a mud mix of water and clay. It must have been a watercourse which had been filed with recent rain. The combination was much worse to dig out than the usual soft sand and it took us an hour of digging to get the truck free. After a while the desert started to become noticeably more fertile with infrequent wisps of straw-like grass sticking up here and there. At sunset we met another lorry heading in the opposite direction to us so we all halted to take tea and share a meal of couscous before continuing into the night. Many scrubby bushes loomed out of the darkness and I realised that we must at last be out of the desert proper and entering the Sahel, the vast region of semi-fertile scrub which lies below the Sahara and stretches in a band from Mauritania to the Horn of Africa. Later in the night we halted to sleep on the soft soil beside the truck.

An amazing dawn chorus of softly cooing doves woke us gently form our slumbers. It was like paradise found after the nothingness of the desert as I glanced around at the surrounding scrub of thick thorn bushes, some with flowers, and small acacia trees. Continuing southwards we passed small clusters of nomadic herder settlements consisting of two or three camel-skin tents and small boys herding hundreds of goats; occasionally we passed Tuareg men perched high on their beautiful white camel mounts. These people have very fine features with hawk-like noses and eagle-like eyes staring out of dark sockets from the white head scarfs. They all had silver hilted daggers in their belts of their blue robes and every second one would sport also a full-length sword.

Later that morning in the middle of nowhere and with no tracks of any certain direction to follow, Musman stopped the truck and sullenly said that they were not going to Agadez after all but were on their way to some village 100km from Agadez and that I should unload the bike and everything else. I was completely taken aback as that had not been our arrangement at all. How on earth was I to find my way through this vast trackless scrubland to Agadez in any event? He then said that Milwaukie would come and guide me to the tarmac road from Arlit to Agadez. I was a bit fed up with the pace of the lorry at this stage and certainly tired of drinking their water, let alone eating bad camel meat, so agreed to take my leave. There really was nothing I could do about their change of direction. At least there were a fair number of nomads in this fertile part of the Sahel so that if I did get lost, I would probably be able to find food, water and hospitality.

The immediate problem was how to safely unload the motorcycle. The first attempt was made by me looping my length of sash cord around her front forks but when the rear wheel was dangling precariously over the side of the 12ft drop to the ground it became obvious that serious damage would occur to the machine and injury to those below were we to continue to offload in this manner.

We hauled the bike back on board and agreed to look for a more suitable place to unload, perhaps another mound or rise in the ground could be found. After half an hour we came across a set of tracks which led to a dry riverbed. The tracks reassured me as they were numerous and possibly would lead to the tar highway to Agadez or at least a small town. At the edge of the riverbed we decided to dig holes in the dried-up sandy riverbank and to reverse the lorry into the riverbed and on into the holes in the bank thus lowering the lorry's height to the top of the bank. This worked a treat and we were able to reduce the offloading height to manageable utilising the sand ladders once more as an inclined ramp. Slowly the four of us lowered the bike down the ramp whilst the fat owner squatted under a nearby tree smoking cigarettes and fiddled with his fat fingers. I gestured for him to join in and help but was ignored. The trickiest bit of the operation was keeping the bike upright on the ramp and my heart was in my mouth for the fear of dropping her. After the job was accomplished, I shook hands all around and exclaimed "Formidable" several times in my schoolboy French.

Oh how nasty fate can be, what goes around, comes around! The lorry was now bogged down in the sand bank holes we had dug, and after much digging and burying of sand ladders the prop shaft sheared off the truck. The connecting plate just tore off all the way around its holding bolts, and that was that for the truck!

I started to repair the puncture on my rear wheel from four days before and installed my very last remaining inner tube into the tyre, paying particular attention not to pinch it whilst there was enough daylight remaining. Some passing nomads sold us a goat, which was quickly dispatched, and we were eating it in a delicious stew within an hour of its slaughter. It was a wonderful contrast to the putrefied camel stew we had survived on up until then.

That night with the early rising crescent of a new moon was another wonderful experience with brilliant starlight reflecting off the surrounding white flanks of the camels belonging to the Tuareg whose goat we had eaten together. The polished silver hilts of their daggers glinted wickedly and in my imagination I could see that they could be drawn in an instance were any offence to be made. A proud and noble people indeed. Stumbling away from the fireside I felt a very sharp shoot of pain in my right foot as if a red-hot needle had been plunged into it. In the starlight I made out the shape of a large camel thorn protruding from my boot. It had pierced through the thick side of my leather boot as if it had been made of butter. God help me, I thought, if I were to run over one of these next day, for Suzy was on her last tube and there was an unknown distance to go across uncertain terrain. It would mean either abandonment or pushing her all the way to Agadez.

As I rejoined the fire I noticed that the atmosphere had become tense and everyone glanced at me uncomfortably. The fat greasy owner stroking his beard challenged with, "How much can you pay me now for your ride? You have damaged my dates with leaking oil from the motorbike and now you must also pay for this breakdown; it was all your fault and it will cost me a lot of money."

Charming, I thought, but as the dice were definitely not loaded in my favour I realised that I had better not upset them but play along as diplomatically as I could.

"How much do you want?" I asked.

"How much will you give?" was the answer.

I said, "It is for you to say."

"Very well $150 US in cash," he demanded.

"Merde," I replied, "that is ridiculous, others pay $60 for a lift all the way from Tamanrasset to Agadez and do not forget that you broke your agreement and that I had to ride the first 250km. Now you cannot take me all the way to Agadez I will offer you $75 and no more for the trip.

"No, I insist on $140 and that is my last price."

I replied, "Very well, I will pay $80 and that is my last offer." I could see that the fat Arab was a past master at the art of bargaining and this was proved by his next ploy, in which he played on my sense of decency.

"You can pay me $120 or nothing, I refuse to accept anything less."

With that he strolled off into the darkness to sit at another fire. Feeling that there could well be trouble brewing if I did not agree to a settlement, I asked Musman to go to him and offer $110. After twenty minutes of discussion Musman came back to say that the offer was acceptable to which I heaved a sigh of relief. As I counted out the dollars, I remembered that I only had $20 bills and thus could only give $120 anyway. Everyone at the fire rolled around with laughter except for Fat Man. I demanded he give me some cigarettes and some CFA francs, the local currency of Niger, which he begrudgingly agreed to, thus all was finally settled.

As a thank you to Musman as he was a decent fellow in sharp contrast to his boss, I gave him a small transistor radio with which he was delighted.

Before the dawn I loaded Suzy up and miraculously managed to fit Milwaukie and the broken truck's drive plate on board. This was achieved by my half sitting on the petrol tank and Milwaukie's bony lap.

Slowly we rolled forward in first gear then changed up to second, but no higher, for should we run into sand we would certainly have overbalanced. Milwaukie guided me with no hesitation through the scrub bush until we encountered the tar road from Arlit without any incidents. That ride was memorable for me because of the soft light of dawn which illuminated the scenery with a thousand different shades of pink heralding the sunrise. The Sahel bush was full of grazing goats, donkeys, sheep and camels with the air full of the sound of cooing doves. At the tar strip I dropped Milwaukie off to lighten my load. He would no doubt get a lift into town from the next vehicle to pass. The remaining 55km to Agadez was a very picturesque run and I noticed for the first time that the locals were not all of Arabic bearing but of darker skin and more rounded in their facial features, for me the start of Black Africa.

At Agadez I changed some money, registered my arrival at the police station and checked for post at the post office. I had given my parents a list of major towns and approximate dates that I was hoping to pass through, and they would write three to four weeks in advance of my collection from the poste restante counter of each. I would frequently mail postcards and also aero mail letters to home with my news. A system of communication which worked fairly well for us.

After a very refreshing ice-cold Coca-Cola I was driving down the main street when I experienced a big jolt from behind with the sound of collision. Glancing around I saw a Tuareg boy lying in the road beside his moped. Obviously, he had not been looking where he was going and unaccountably had just run into the back of me. I stopped as quickly as I could and walked back to see if he was OK. As I approached, he jumped up, eyes staring out of his head in terror and in one bound streaked off like lightening on his moped. After glancing at his rapidly disappearing figure up the road I turned around and noticed a large chunk had been taken out of my sleeping bag roll. If it had not been there to cushion the blow of the impact, the damage might have been much more serious.

A few kilometres outside of Agadez there was a campsite and after setting up my tent I met Jean, a Frenchman who had spent the past twelve years travelling by bicycle in Africa.

Jean – twelve years on his bicycle in Africa, a great cook and con artist!

He had a steady stream of interesting and amusing tales to tell, especially about the girls in Zaire who he found climbing through his hotel room window to reach him after he had retired for an early night's sleep, having locked his bedroom door.

In the centre of the campsite was a murky and slimy green swimming pool; this was a great attraction to all who stayed there, and some considered it to be the finest feature in all of Agadez. Many an afternoon was to be passed swimming and idling away the heat of the day on the edge of that pool.

Back in the town later in the day to my joy I was able to locate some more spare inner tubes. These were 2.25 x 18 rather than the correct size of 3.25 x 18 but I figured that they would work OK in the absence of any other option and so ordered four to be collected in the morning.

On my ride back to camp on the rough gravel piste one of the four metal tube struts that held my rear top box in position had cracked all the way through. The next day after collecting the new inner tubes I found without difficulty a welding shop; the manager waved me inside and the work area was cleared of old bedframes etc. The workshop's welding equipment looked to be highly dangerous to say the least. It was an electric arc welder with a power connecting lead which had been patched up in several places with layers of insulating tape. An hour later an excellent repair job had been undertaken with much beating of metal and showers of sparks. A couple of old iron pipes had been cut to length, split open and then welded around each of the carrier frame's tubes where cracks were apparent to form a splint repair.

Back at camp a Danish traveller set my blood curdling with a tale from Southern Nigeria. An Italian had been driving to Lagos in a Land Rover. He came across what he thought was a police checkpoint (these are very frequently encountered in Nigeria apparently). However, the roadblock turned out to be manned by bandits and when they discovered that the Italian had not much in the way to give them, they cut off his hand. After hearing this tale, I decided that Southern Nigeria was to be avoided at all cost and later other travellers' tales confirmed that this was a good decision.

The next morning Jean had packed up all his belongings and obligingly posed for a photo before cycling the 7km to town. He had found a job in one of the less salubrious hotels run by a French girl married to a Nigerian. He had to paint the hotel's restaurant chairs and do various plumbing jobs. I learnt that Jean had funded most of his past twelve years by "borrowing" and doing handyman's jobs, no doubt greatly appreciated by the many expats all over the continent. I never did see the £10 he persuaded me to loan him on the strength of a friend repaying a loan back to him later that particular day!

Agadez campsite

I had planned to leave later that afternoon but was not feeling well by the time afternoon came. My stomach was heaving with persistent cramps and I felt feverish and had a severe headache too. A young German driving a Mercedes truck with a Peugeot on the back, planned for sale in Cameroon, came over and started chatting. When he heard how groggy I felt he explained that he was a psychologist and that if I trusted him, he could cure me. I was somewhat sceptical but having nothing to lose I agreed to be his guinea pig. First, he made me lie face down on my sleeping mat and then told me to relax all of my muscles and to clear my mind of all thoughts except what he was saying. Gently he asked me to imagine a blank green wall, smooth and uniform. When I told him I could visualise this he asked me to see an orange ball in front of the wall. This was extremely difficult to visualise. Finally, I got it and became totally immersed with the effort to sustain the picture. After a few minutes I heard him telling me to forget the image and to turn over onto my back and rest. Five minutes later I sat up and felt perfectly normal and fit. I tried to find out from him how this had happened but all I could get out of him was that he had used a process similar to hypnosis.

The following afternoon after a lazy few hours by the pool I packed up and took the piste for the final time down and through Agadez, where just outside the town I felt a cool spray on my left knee. Stopping to investigate I found that my collapsible polythene water bag had sprung a leak, so I inverted it in its canvas bag holder and carried on. As the sun dropped lower in the sky, I decided to risk sunburn and took off my shirt. Bareback riding was a definite pleasure in that temperature; a cool breeze enveloped me, interrupted now and again by the suicidal impact of some insect or other. The road south of Agadez was brilliant being only four months old and a rare treat. Sunset was awesome again with a gentle tinge of gold remaining in the sky long after the fiery globe had vanished. Two hours later I guided Suzy off the road and out across the Sahel sands to an open tract of bush-free country to pass the night. No longer was the moon with us but this made the starlight even brighter and the heavens glistened as alive with jewels. Occasionally a shooting star would streak across the sky or a satellite would carve its preordained track across the vast dome of the universe.

We left at dawn and about ten miles later I was startled to hear the clatter of hooves. Looking to my left I noticed a small gazelle bounding along the road beside me at a surprising speed, about 40mph. As I braked, the buck gracefully flew off the road and disappeared, leaping into the scrubby bush. What a wonderful experience to start the day with. Later I passed small herds of cattle with long and dangerous looking V-shaped horns and also herds of camels, goats and donkeys. With every passing mile the surrounding bush was becoming greener and more fertile with numerous watering holes and small lakes, each alive with an abundance of coloured birds. This really was one of the most picturesque stretches of bush country I was to see anywhere in Africa. By lunchtime I had reached the regional cattle town of Tahoua (403kms from Agadez) where I explored the well-stocked fruit and vegetable market piled high with things I could not put any name to. On the town square I found a little restaurant with a menu pinned up on its front mud wall in French with prices alongside. Within a few minutes of ordering rice and meat, a steaming mountain was placed in front of me along with a very grubby spoon which I rejected in favour of my fingers in the local custom. I always felt that my hands were less likely to carry infection than dirty thumb-polished cutlery. After this meal as I passed a small shack an old wizened man beckoned me to come in, offering me a glass of whitish-looking liquid from his paraffin-powered refrigerator. This he told me was "Boule" and seemed to taste of sour milk and wheatgerm. My host recommended this brew particularly for its fortifying and aphrodisiac properties, being greatly prized by the locals of Tahoua.

I took my leave of these friendly inhabitants and rode on for my target of the Nigerian border and then onwards to Sokoto where Errol and Jaqueline had invited me to stay.

After half an hour it was still uncomfortably hot so I spotted a shady tree beside a lake and pulled under it, laid out my sleeping mat for a rest and within ten minutes was surrounded by a group of small boys who had sprung up from seemingly nowhere with their smiling faces and gleaming white teeth flashing in the sun. After attempting to ignore them and rest for an hour I opened my eyes to see that they were waiting patiently by me in the shade longing to talk. Out of courtesy I answered their questions put in bad French and answered even more haltingly in my faltering Africanised argot.

Having hopefully satisfied them I took to the road once more and by 5pm arrived at the border town of Birnin-Konni. The customs officials were very polite and courteous to me as I passed out of Niger, the complete reverse of the attitude of the Nigerians. Overall, I really enjoyed Niger.

Chapter 9

NIGERIA

THE OFFICERS SPENT ABOUT TWO HOURS QUESTIONING ME IN MINUTE DETAIL IN a fairly unwelcoming manner. Possibly they were unfamiliar with the ten-day visa I had been begrudgingly granted by their embassy back in London; also I had no doubt that they were assessing me for the possibility of extraction of a bribe. I remained polite, cool and collected as I had plenty to be found in undeclared currency and documents identifying my final destination as South Africa would not be well received.

At last everything was declared to be in order and I rode off into the gathering dusk. I was soon struck by the craziness of Nigeria; every vehicle seemed to be driven at top speed by unskilled first-generation drivers lusting for speed. In the mere 150m to Sokoto I passed dozens of upturned vehicles and burned-out wrecks littering the roadside. Many crowded vans rushed up behind me and then swerved out madly at the last second to overtake me only to fiercely cut back in on me the moment that they were by. Just outside of Sokoto there were a couple of police checkpoints to be passed. At the first one I was waved through with a courteous nod. At the second one before a Bailey bridge over the river a rather tipsy sergeant waited for me but after a few questions lost interest; I think I was delaying his next drink so I decided not to compliment him on his ex-British army 303 which was being waved around with gay abandon.

At the Roads Nigeria depot, a young lad willingly guided me on a moped to Errol's house. In no time at all Errol was greeting me effusively and ensured that liberal amounts of ice-cold beer were flowing down my dust-parched throat. Jaqueline prepared a traditional Surinam-style supper with all sorts of exotic dishes finishing with banana fritters. Also staying with them at the house was a young couple from Holland who had driven across the desert in a Peugeot 504 to sell in Cameroon. Their crossing had not been without incident. They got lost on the tricky bit of no road between Tamanrasset and In Guezzam in a sandstorm. When the storm had abated there were no evident tracks to follow and their car was severely bogged down in soft sand. Ben had left his wife alone in the car and carrying just one litre of water had walked off in what he thought was the right direction of the main route. By chance a couple of hours later he was found by an Algerian army patrol who then set out to rescue his wife and the car. "Never again," Ben kept repeating.

My sleeping quarters was the living room floor, which was beautifully air-conditioned; in the middle of the night I was woken by a scuffling noise and turned over to see that one of Errol's pet hedgehogs had got into the room and was drinking from my glass of water by my head. I nearly burst out laughing having expected to encounter a rat. In the morning I took a lift into town with Ben to cash some money. Only at the third bank we tried were we able to exchange some travellers' cheques and then at a poor rate of exchange. Later I did a much more lucrative deal with a Pakistani businessman standing next to me in the bank trying to get finance for an upcoming trip to Europe. Both sitting in Ben's car, I exchanged $20 with him for 40 naira instead of the 25 naira offered by the bank. The bank transaction had taken two hours, this trade had taken just five minutes.

After a very pleasant couple of days' "R&R" at Sokoto with my excellent hosts I was once again getting the itch to move on further across this exciting dark continent. Errol very kindly arranged for Suzy to be topped up with petrol at his expense at the road depot's petrol pump and also made arrangements for me to stay at his company's house in Kano. Plus, a fuel chit was issued to me to refuel the bike at the company's depot halfway from here to Kano, all incredibly generous and much appreciated.

The countryside was very populated and fertile on this stretch of road, similar to the English countryside on a hot midsummer's day in appearance in some places, with oak-like trees and then every so often some very un-English baobab trees. These trees are most unusual in appearance as though they were standing upside down on their heads with their roots growing out of their tops instead of branches. At ground level the trunk is extremely thick and tapers halfway up its length.

Frequent small townships lined the road with many stalls selling a great variety of merchandise. I even noticed some Suzuki signs; however, the largest motorcycle I saw apart from the police bikes were just 200cc, there being an import restriction on any machine with a larger cylinder capacity. Consequently, many a Nigerian biker was amazed by the size of Suzy's engine, a typical remark being, "You have a very strong motorcycle, sir!"

Outside Kano I ran into five police roadblocks all with a pole across the highway; at each one I was politely waved through with no questions asked despite my rear number plate being partially obscured by my suspended tent roll, which I had repositioned for a lower centre of gravity.

It was with a fair degree of exhaustion that I completed the 350-mile trip and hit the thick and furious mad traffic of downtown Kano with fumes choking me from a thousand mopeds. A cacophony of horns and screaming motors. Thank goodness the Roads Nigeria guest house was able to accommodate me in air-conditioned comfort; the only other apparent option would have been the Central Hotel, a notorious pick-up spot for girls of the night and not cheap at $80 a night!

The lodge boy cooked me an excellent breakfast after which my first priority was a call at the post office where to my delight there were three letters waiting for me in poste restante. The old city itself I found to be not very impressive; perhaps it was all too frenetic for my liking, reminding me of New Delhi but with far fewer beggars and fewer street vendors. I visited the Emir's Palace but also came away uninspired.

The following day I made a trip out to a leprosy hospital ten miles outside Kano at Yadakunya, which I had previously heard about. This turned out to be a most interesting and worthwhile visit.

THE YADAKUNYA LEPROSY HOSPITAL

It was 11am by the time that I had found the route to the hospital and was winding my way along the 12km of sandy track to reach it. A group of men shabbily dressed sitting under the shade of a tree shouted and welcomed my arrival. I looked a second time as I had detected something unusual about them, and then I realised that some of the hands waving were devoid of fingers. I swallowed a bit with surprise and realised that I must be nearing my destination. Sure enough, around the next bend appeared a cluster of neatly laid out buildings surrounded by plenty of shade. A few patients were sitting around on chairs out in the sunshine; I spotted the main entrance and pulled up alongside it. A grinning face greeted me with "Welcome, master". I explained that I had come to see Dr Tom Koorn; he was out but his assistant Max appeared and was very interested in my Oxfam sponsorship venture. A few minutes later Dr Koorn pulled up in his VW van. We shook hands and I explained the reason for my visit and my quest to raise money for the treatment of leprosy. He immediately invited me to coffee and a chat at his lovely cottage half a mile away. I told him what little I knew about leprosy and he gave me a brief and detailed lecture about the disease and about the problems that they were faced with at Kaduna with their treatment.

He told me that leprosy was a bacterial disease; since the 1960s there had been an increasing resistance to the standard treatment drug called Dapsone. This drug had been used as the standard go-to treatment extensively since 1947 and was fairly cheap to obtain. Leprosy cannot be casually transmitted despite the medieval belief that this was so, which resulted in the horrific leper colonies and complete isolation from surrounding society, Incubation is over a long period of several years and the first symptom of the disease is a lump on the skin with discolouration; then follows bone absorption with muscular atrophy and nerve deterioration. There is no form of leper rehabilitation after cure in Nigeria where in any event there are too many victims to treat. The estimate for Nigeria was six people infected per 10,000 and only one in six of those infected would receive any form of treatment. These numbers were now decreasing due to improved education, hygiene and communication. But the lack of interest and awareness of the modern Western world to leprosy due to its lack of prevalence outside the Third World meant that not much funding was available for further research and treatment projects to be undertaken. It was really viewed as just another Third World issue.

After this chat we returned to the hospital and Max took me first into the diagnostic laboratory where analysis of smears took place to find out the extent of the disease and to monitor its response to treatment. Some cases can take up to seven years to cure.

We then went into the wards and I saw a variety of patients, some in the early stages of the disease and some in the advanced later stages. I hoped my shock as to their condition did not reveal itself. The patients were so quiet, dignified and as resigned to their fate as sick animals; looking into their eyes was the saddest part of all, for most had not a spark of hope therein, just a forlorn look of hopelessness, reflecting as "Let Allah's will be done."

Most of the very serious cases knew that even should the disease be arrested, they would never be able to lead a normal life again. I saw men with no eyelids, women with no legs, all had deformed hands, many without toes and others riddled with various infections.

They told me that children usually are not separated from their mothers until the age of five as the incubation period is over a long term, up to ten years, so it is considered to be best for the psychology of the child to maintain proximity and contact with their parents. Dr Tom explained to me how he performed plastic surgery on patients who had suffered bone erosion and also how he had reattached tendons to remaining digits in order to achieve some mobility. He also showed me a patient who had new eyelids and demonstrated a blinking exercise to retrain the eyelids, which was fairly successful. He said that physiotherapy treatment could bring enormous benefit to his patients but unfortunately in Nigeria at this time there was a complete absence of this service. He acknowledged that there was a point reached in the advanced stage of the disease when further treatment was of no use.

Dr Tom had been at Yadakunya Hospital for the past four years and was very immersed in his world. After this distressing but informative tour he extended an invitation to lunch to me, which I gratefully accepted. At lunch I talked with him about cannibalism, which he assured me was still prevalent in parts of Nigeria except in the Muslim-practising Northern Territory. As evidence he mentioned each year more than 200 children disappeared without trace from the streets of Kano. He also talked about the religious riots of last Christmas, which had taken several lives but for political purposes were not reported on. Dr Tom saw with his own eyes some 1500 corpses lying in the police barracks yard and more trucks incoming piled high with more bodies as he had been called there to treat an injured policeman. The army had been very ruthless with the mobs, simply opening fire with all weapons at their disposal. Overall, he estimated more than 2000 people were killed. This seemed to me to have been the most brutal suppression of any riot I had ever heard of and it sent a chill down my spine; I resolved to get out of Kano as soon as possible.

After lunch I returned to the hospital to take a few photos and then left for Kano with much food for thought.

The next morning the steward brought me an extra-large breakfast, a reward for my compliments to him the previous evening on the quality of the cooking. For the first time I had to buy some petrol in Nigeria and had a very pleasant surprise: it cost 60p per gallon and that was at the official rate of exchange; at my black market rate that converted to only 30p, happy motoring indeed.

At lunchtime I attempted to picnic under some fairly thick shrubs but soon discovered that thousands of flies and other insects had decided to "chop" (Nigerian slang for eat) me.

The road to Bauchi got rough in places as it was in the course of being upgraded from a gravel piste to a tarmac highway. At one village where I stopped, I was immediately surrounded by inquisitive children so to maintain popularity I dipped into my front haversack and pulled out some wrapped sweets and a couple of biro pens for grateful distribution. As evening approached, I branched off the highway and onto a narrow road signed 80km for Yankari Game Reserve and its camp at Wikki warm springs. In 1981, this was one of a very few wildlife reserves of any significance remaining in Nigeria and held game in a smaller area than any other national reserve on the continent. The sad fact was that Nigerian wildlife had been completely decimated by explosive population growth and the legacy of the Biafran conflict down south twelve years before, which had put paid to most of the country's game.

Nigeria in previous times must have been extremely populous in wildlife for the land is very fertile. Man's greed and hunger for meat for the pot has eliminated most of it.

The narrow road approaching the reserve was tarred and wound its way agreeably up and down through some lovely bush country to the lodge of Wikki Springs with huge red termite mounds standing sometimes as tall as trees. The hot springs emerged out of the base of a cliff and a pool had been made for swimming where it emerged. On one side of it was a concrete walkway and on the other the jungle came right down to the edge of the clear blue water. As I swam in the pleasantly warm water to my amazement a couple of baboons strolled down to the water's edge to drink. The descent of a couple of well-endowed Nigerian mamas into the pool was my cue to leave rather rapidly as they both most suggestively approached me with a very obvious intent!

Despite the poor game-viewing prospects, I was able to squeeze into the back of an overcrowded Safari truck for the evening game drive. We encountered a reasonable variety of buffalo, buck, storks, kites, a few groups of baboons and a single elephant over the next hour and a half.

Heading away on the road once more there was a spectacular view of the highlands of Cameroon; these are beautiful ranges of volcanic-shaped mountains dotted with green vegetation and huge granite boulders. Agriculture is the prime industry and I passed many villages alongside the road with large herds of fat cattle. The population was so dense that it was proving almost impossible to find a quiet and hidden stop to make camp that evening and I was forced to ride for longer than I had wished for. Eventually in the dark I found a dried-up riverbed and erected my tent under one of its earthen banks, praying that the rains would not break that night upriver, as I would have been inundated in a flash flood in no time, not very sensible. As soon as my tent was up the mosquitos commenced a most violent bombardment, squadron after squadron dive-bombed me, biting savagely right through my Wranglers. Many must have entered with me through the tent flap as I dived in to escape. Inside the tent I erected my ex-military green mosquito net hung from the front and rear poles but still did not entirely preclude them as I lay sweating in the heat of the now airless night.

The road to Yola rose steeply uphill again through the most delightful rolling countryside. At the town I stopped for a posh restaurant lunch as a treat and had a superb bowl of rice and stewed chicken served by a waiter smartly dressed in an impeccable white jacket whilst I admired the view over the town from its sixth-floor balcony.

Riverbed Camp

After leaving Yola I tried to find a small unmapped road which I had been told would take me to Cameroon. After 20km of riding the road deteriorated to a small sandy track and on a bend I had my worst fall to date at about 30mph; fortunately the sand was soft with no gravel so no real damage was done to machine or rider apart from a severe shake up and the bursting of the zip on my tank bag. I would now be faced for the rest of the journey with the possibility of stealthy hands creeping into the sides of the bag and retrieving whatever they could find; despite my fears, over the months to come I lost nothing from that bag. A few passers-by helped me to pick the bike up and reload. Also, I was told that although the track did cross the border to Cameroon there was a big river to be forded and also no Nigerian border post to process me out of the country. That information made me turn around and head back to Yola, planning a border crossing further north of the town, for I did not want to lose my carnet de passage customs bond for the machine. This was issued by the AA and was set at $800 although back in the UK this five-year-old machine was probably only worth £200.

Outside Yola was a long bridge over the river and another branch road leading to Cameroon, which unfortunately I missed and only realised that had been the case many

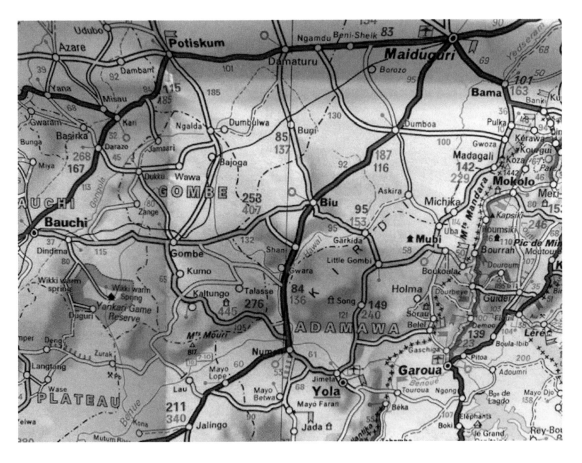

kilometres further on. I consulted the map again and found another customs post marked at a place called Mubi and a village called Sahuda.

As I passed through Sahuda I saw that the whole village was out watching a football match on the local pitch. A young man on a moped tried to wave me down, but without appearing to take notice I carried on rolling up an incline towards the border barrier. Ten minutes later this same young man caught me up and it turned out importantly for me that he was the post's immigration officer. Fortunately, he was not at all put out by my ignoring him back in the village. It happened that he was also the son of the chief immigration officer and to demonstrate his power he suddenly ordered an officer apparently more senior to him, and twice his age, to stop processing my documentation and to lower the flag outside the post. Five minutes later, order performed, the officer duly returned to complete my emigration. The lad advised me that the Cameroonians were unlikely to be manning their post at this hour and kindly invited me to return to sleep at his post were that to be the case.

I must add at this stage that relations between Nigeria and Cameroon were not at their best, as a Nigerian border patrol had been attacked and taken out by a Cameroonian patrol only the week before as they had accidentally strayed across the border. Surprisingly here though the atmosphere was quiet, friendly and relaxed. Perhaps here no one had heard of the incident although some Nigerian politicians had publicly called for a punitive expedition to be sent against the Cameroonians. Eventually, in pitch darkness I left the border post and ventured into no-man's land delighted that no one had asked for my currency declaration form or had asked for "dash" – the local word for bribe.

Chapter 10

CAMEROON

A T THE CAMEROONIAN BORDER BARRIER NO ONE WAS ON DUTY, SO I RODE around the pole and parked at the front of the customs hut. Here there was another village, a crowd of colourfully dressed people were streaming back across the border from the football match. In no time a crowd of enthusiastic, friendly and smiling youngsters had gathered around me, offering cigarettes, snacks and asking all manner of questions such as "Where are you coming from? Where are you going to? How old are you? How big is your moto?" Some were so amazed to see the bike that they spontaneously would break into dance as they passed by. Then I heard a familiar voice greeting me: it was the young Nigerian immigration official. He said that he had come over to help me. He first offered me another cigarette and then opened up a handkerchief containing some spiced meat and another with samosas. I refused at first, but he was most insistent that I should share the food with him. Then to my complete surprise he suddenly placed 2000 CFA into my hand saying that I must take the money for how could a mzungu (white man) be without it, even for one night in Africa? I was very flabbergasted for this was the equivalent of $8 US but before I could say anything he disappeared into the darkness of the night. The whole incident was incomprehensible to me because I had heard so many tales of Nigerian officials ripping off travellers; to have one chase me over another country's border to give me money was unbelievable! I had the feeling that Cameroon was to be another highlight of the journey.

As the dawn broke, I gathered up my sleeping bag and other belongings from the customs post balcony in preparation for the customs and immigration formalities. Many trucks were crossing over to Nigeria and others were creaking up the gravel road from the

My trusty Olympus Trip

Cameroon Border Village Market

Cameroon Border Village Market

Cameroon Border Village Market

village and on to the Cameroon side. It was also market day and after I cleared customs with a minimum of inconvenience, I was able to take some photographs of the amazing market in action. In contrast to Nigeria the people were completely liberal concerning photography. In some other parts of Africa, it is not easy to take good spontaneous pictures of people for a variety of reasons, such as pride, greed for money or fear that a part of their spirit could be captured and used for witchcraft. Sometimes just to produce a camera is to spoil the atmosphere and scene of what one is trying to capture. My style of photography was trying very much to be one of an observer rather than that of the tourist picture-taker using bribes and coercion. My little Olympus Trip was always close at hand but discreet in its appearance and easy to operate.

The road away from the village was a very rough ungroomed track with high piles of gravel forming inverse cambers on the inside of the bends rather than banking on the outer side to help a vehicle negotiate around the curve. The consequence of this poor road state was to cause me often to slide off the edge of the bend into a scooped ditch grabbing in panic at my brakes and swearing as I fought to regain control. The only compensation for the poor road was the absolutely breathtaking view of range after range of mountains covered in lush green vegetation. By midday I had had two falls, once twisting my leg fairly sharply to remind me of the risks I was taking riding alone on such a road. Otherwise I came to no harm, but the going was hard work.

Eventually after the provincial town of Garoua I struck a decent tarred road once more and towards evening I passed a signpost marked "Campement des Elephants". I was curious and could not resist the urge to explore further so turned around and followed the narrow winding sandy track off into the bush following a set of Land Rover-type tyre tracks. Soon the track became nothing more than two parallel sets of wheel indentations ploughing through the thick bush scrub. Obviously, this track was little used and in some places the path was grown over by bush. I began to wonder what the hell I would do were I to come face to face with an elephant. After nearly 10km of crawling along at 5–10mph I noticed some fresh bicycle tracks in the sand and that reassured me and relieved me slightly of my fears, thinking how much more vulnerable a man on a bicycle would be to wild animals than myself on a noisy machine. Also, from these tracks I deduced that there must be people living somewhere around here. A few minutes later I rounded a bend and saw riding ahead the cyclist; he spoke no English or French but nevertheless was very friendly and happy to meet me on this rather lonely trail. After breaking the ice with a shared cigarette, I continued ahead of him but with having no more fresh bicycle marks to follow in the sand, within five minutes I was thrown off the bike in a patch of soft sand. As the bike was slightly angled in a direction of righting, I made a superhuman effort and succeeded in lifting her upright without prior unloading. This discovery that I could in the right situation after all find the strength to lift her back up when loaded saved a great deal of time on future falls and bolstered my self-confidence.

An hour after turning off the safe tar road onto this nightmarish bush track a small collection of African huts came into sight and at a fork in the pathway a group of boys willingly pointed me on down the track away from the safety and companionship of the village on to the encampment 5km further down the track. When I made it there it turned out to be a very run-down rondavel with flaking whitewashed walls and decayed thatched roof; it must have been abandoned years before. It was centred in a clearing in the bush from which there was an arresting view over the bush to a sandy riverbank. As I smoked and admired the scene, still astride the bike, I suddenly heard a loud rumbling sound coming from some deep bushes in front of me and then I felt the spooky presence of something large and potentially hostile observing me and yet I could not see anything. I dismounted and tried to open the door of the round hut, but it was locked, as were the windows too. Not relishing the idea of setting up my tent outside on my own and definitely unsettled by the mysterious presence, I decided to return to the village to see if there might be a key for the hut held there.

As I strolled down to have another look at the river and to see if I could see any trace of the beast whose presence I suspected, another loud deep rumble came from the bushes and then a rustling in the undergrowth made me run back to the clearing and jump on Suzy. Kicking her off as a madman I scuttled out of the clearing and down the track towards the village with the fear of the unknown behind spurring me on.

Halfway back to the village I heard another strange noise, this time coming from the rear of the bike, and glancing around observed that my white rear carrier was again about to fall off as the welding done back in Agadez had fractured in all four supporting bars. At the track junction to the village the few boys I had seen before were gathered playing with a toy which was universally popular all over Africa from Morocco to South Africa. It was a model of a car or a lorry made from wire and wood with a steering column projecting out of the roof of the model attached to the front wheel axle so that it could be pushed and steered at the same time. As I approached, they abandoned play; one of them had a few words of French and I was able to explain that the camp rondavel was locked and that I also needed help to repair my luggage frame. With a smile he said that I should follow him to the village and speak with the headman. Under a large tree in the village clearing were three or four men all squatting in a circle. One of them sported a rather fine red fez-like hat and had finer features than the others. I walked up to him with outstretched hand which he firmly grasped and to my surprise replied to my greeting in French with some pidgin English. He explained that in earlier days he had been a policeman in the English part of what was now Cameroon close to south-east Nigeria.

As soon as I had explained my predicament, he gave a command and a couple of bystanders scuttled off and returned a few minutes later with some stout old bolts and cut strips of rubber from the inner tube of a lorry. This he told me was "catou" and would easily fix the carrier. Ten minutes later both sides of the carrier were splinted and firmly bound. This "catou" was used extensively by Africans all over the continent for all manner of repairs and was available for purchase in nearly every market I visited, often with a dedicated stall. The repair having been completed and cigarettes dispensed to all concerned, I was motioned by the headman to follow a man who led me around a couple of huts into a secluded courtyard. He said that it was his hut and told me I could have use of it for the night. It was getting dark by then, so I was grateful for his offer. Together we went back to the bike to collect my luggage; when we got back to the hut he disappeared and reappeared with an old iron bed assisted by another, which they placed in the courtyard for my use.

They eagerly helped me to suspend my mosquito net above it, which was greatly admired. Next a basin of water and a bar of soap were brought to me. It was fantastic to wash off the day's accumulated dirt, dust and squashed flies from my body and to give my feet a cleansing soak. Whilst I was washing, a wooden armchair had been placed in the courtyard and as soon as I had freshened up, I was made to sit in the chair and a large bowl of rice and meat was served to me with a smaller bowl of delicious maize biscuits. Respectfully, they retired to allow me to feed unobserved. It was by now pitch dark but my courtyard was lit by a thoughtfully placed hurricane lamp, which provided adequate light to read by and for me to write my page-a-day diary up, without which I now forty years later would be unable to recount the saga of that day or many others of the trip.

After a while I strolled out of the hut to investigate what was happening in the village. I found all the men sitting in a long line quietly talking in front of a large fire. The women and children sat in a wide circle around another fire a little distance away. It seemed that some special event was taking place that night. Instinctively, I realised that they would have invited me to join them had they wished me to be present. I retired quietly to my iron-framed bed back in the courtyard and slept. It was about 10.30pm when I was awakened with the sound of young boys' voices chanting and I heard the loud refrain "Allah Akbar" repeated many times. The chanting went on and on, waxing and waning, verse after verse of what I took to be the Koran as a full moon hung in the crystal-clear heavens; I lay awake for hours mesmerised by the harmonies of the chanting. Sometimes it would be just the boys singing, then the girls from their fire, then to be taken up by the men and women whose voices would swell to join in a chorus or two. Sparks from the fires were flying over my courtyard as the fires were stoked up from time to time. At first light I was amazed to still hear the boys singing, repeating their verses of the Koran. They had been at it all night and only ceased at sunrise.

As I prepared to leave and was strapping on my numerous bags to the bike, what seemed like half the village turned up to wave me off. I gratefully shook the headman's hand and gave him a big smile of genuine appreciation and profuse thanks for the village's amazing hospitality. It was a full hour of very careful riding back down the track to the tar highway and then on to Ngaoundéré, the regional capital, where I stopped at a roadside shack restaurant for more rice and meat.

Leaving, I had difficulty in finding the route out of town for the main road onwards to Garoua Bolai, where the road forks left for the Central African Republic or right for the capital, Yaoundé. Eventually a guy on an ancient moped led me out to the correct road, or more accurately to be described as a very rocky and rough bush track, which gave both bike and rider a good shake up for the next few hours. As I rounded one bend on a downhill stretch a herd of cattle blocked my route. I slowed up and at the last minute they decided not to make way for me but to hold their ground. I jammed on both brakes and the front wheel slid on the dirt and down we tumbled on to the warm red earth. Rubbing my knee, I rose slowly, vehemently cursing these lazy beasts.

Towards evening we were still in rolling hill country, thick with villages lining the route. In most of Africa it struck me that most people live by a road or track but for the nomadic tribes and the pygmies of the deep jungle, largely because of the vast distances and nature of the terrain.

I found a good place to camp behind an abandoned overturned shell of a lorry and cooked up a vegetable soup using some potatoes etc. that I had brought in a market that afternoon. It was really good to have some hot food after a long day's haul. My little petrol fuel stove was an invaluable asset and to me, worth its weight in gold. It could be quite dangerous when it was starting up from cold, sending out scorching clouds of burning pressurised petrol. I treated it as a firework on start-up, light and stand well back! Frequently the jet would be blocked with residue and it had to be regularly cleared with a darning needle, but it served me extremely well over the several months of the journey.

The road continued to be as rough as ever with bad and bumpy corrugations, except for one luxurious stretch of about 2km leading over a river via a Bailey bridge. It was difficult to understand the logic of this stretch as from thereon to Garoua Bolai, the road/track was every bit as bad as before. But then Africa is full of things to puzzle over. On the rough, muddy, dirty trail, the most important thing I learnt was to always keep my

Cameroon Jungle track towards Yaoundé

eyes on the road surface and to read it. If vehicle tracks started to zigzag, one pretty much knew that there would be trouble ahead. Because of this it was often difficult to see the passing scenery as invariably when my eyes were off the road I would fly bounding and cursing over a series of potholes. Intense concentration was required to avoid these, an hour's riding would fly by as a few minutes and there was certainly no time in which to get bored; the effort needed to stay safe was too great for that. Boredom on the road only set in much later on my journey on the ultra-smooth highways of South Africa where the distances between towns are vast and the dry plains of the Karoo stretch endlessly on to the horizon.

At midday I rode in to Garoua Bolai, stopped for lunch and then decided not to carry on straight away to the Central African Republic as I wanted to explore Cameroon further. After leaving town, the track deteriorated even further, as being the main route of everything from the C.A.R. to Yaoundé and then on to the port of Doala, it was greatly worn out by a continual stream of often weighty traffic. Due to this I was forced to slow down to a snail's pace, which was just as well because there were some monster potholes to be dodged, any one of which, had I hit it, could have buckled a wheel or worse. As the shadows grew longer and the surrounding jungle denser it became difficult to see where I was going. At sunset I looked for a suitable place to camp for the night and having spotted a seemingly little-used turn-off, pulled off the main track and set up my camp using Suzy's headlight to see what I was doing. As I unstrapped my sleeping bag, mat and tent I discovered that my tent pegs were missing from inside the rolled-up tent, probably having been shaken out by the rough track corrugations earlier in the day. The sky, as well as being very dark, from what I could see of it was threatening rain, so no tent pegs was a serious issue. As I puffed on yet another cigarette the solution came to me. I used my toolkit to substitute as pegs: screwdrivers, long-nosed pliers, files, spanners, tyre levers, etc. and as a final anchor, I tied the front rope to the bike.

Later I heard laughter coming from further down the track and around the corner came a small party of jungle folk, two young girls and a lad. The latter was carrying a lethal-looking 5ft spear and the girls carried a panga each. As they saw me they stopped dead in their tracks, eyes darting out of their sockets. I called to them, coaxing them over with a waved packet of cigarettes, which put them back in their comfort zone in no time at all, and they broke into smiles and then questions of curiosity. As we smoked in harmony, I asked in my steadily improving but still faltering French why they were carrying weapons. The lad said that he had come through the forest to see his sister safely off to the road and that the spear was to protect them from wild animals. I asked what sort of wild animals they might meet and my best interpretation of his reply of "La Lenu" was possibly a leopard.

As I lay that night in my tent thinking of this mystery beast, I jumped at every sound which came out of the surrounding jungle. At 4am the developing storm broke and my tent was lashed with torrents of rainwater. By first light it was still raining hard but my improvised tent pegs had held good except for a couple which had been torn out by the wind, and remarkably not a single rain drop had penetrated inside the tent's single-skin cover, a tribute to the quality of the goods made in Hong Kong.

Diary note – it was 19th June 1981 and I had now travelled 7,703 miles from home.

It stopped raining by 7.30am and so I retracted my tools from the ground, shook as much moisture off the tent as I could then packed it up and headed off down the track, which was very wet with many pools of water of unknown depth and slippery in places. At each village dotted along the route the rain barrier poles were all lowered to halt traffic until the road was sufficiently dry, to minimise its further damage. But for me a willing attendant would run out of the adjacent hut and raise it, or else I would just ride around it.

I often wondered what the villagers thought of me as they fleetingly saw me passing in and out of their world. Often, they would break into spontaneous dance to express their wonder at such a strange sight of a white man on an overloaded motorcycle coming from whence and going to where?

Drops of rain splashed more frequently and then painfully onto my face. My visor was by this stage so scratched that when I lowered it my vision was practically zero; even when it was not raining, I only used it to protect my eyes from dust raised from passing vehicles or else in areas where flies were abundant. In spite of this, every day I averaged six to seven flies blown into my eyes, which could be very painful if I was going fast.

The clouds above grew blacker and more ominous and then the heavens opened just as if a bath tap had been turned full on and I was directly underneath it. There was only one thing for it; as I could not see where I was going and the road had become a river, I had to take shelter in the jungle. I left Suzy by the roadside and took shelter in my bright yellow waterproofs under the largest leafed plant that I could find. Even that provided no real protection and within two minutes I was completely soaked. Two hours later, when the torrent ceased, I set off once again for Yaoundé. But half an hour later the deluge returned; this time I was passing through a village and took shelter under the rattan shelter in front of a hut. Amazed looks were given to me by the inhabitants, an old man, a woman and several small children. We had no real words of communication, but my cigarettes were accepted with delight and appreciation. I realised that they were very much overawed by my appearance; they were cooking some sort of yam jungle root over a slow smouldering fire in the centre of the shelter but strangely made no offer of it to me; probably too shy.

An hour later the rain let up once more and I made the town of Bertoua, where I arrived drenched to the skin, shivering and starving. I was surprised to find a reasonably modern hotel there and was able to book a room for just $5, and found some delicious grilled meat in the market to feast upon.

I asked the time from a smartly dressed guy who insisted that I come with him for a beer and took me to a rather dingy bar where Paul disclosed that he was the Commandant of the town's prison; before we parted he made me all but promise on pain of imprisonment that we should meet up the following day.

The road was almost dried out next morning as I left for Yaoundé, some 350km distant. However, where the potholes lay in the water run-offs the mud was extremely sticky and slippery, so great caution was required to safely get past these areas. I passed a petrol tanker which had slewed off the road on a steep hill and was now hopelessly bogged up to its axles in thick mud.

Road blocked

Further on I encountered two lorries which had collided head on into each other completely blocking the road to all but my sort of traffic. The drivers and their passengers informed me gleefully that no one had been killed and would I report the collision to the gendarmes at Nanga-Eboko. So half an hour later I arrived at the police station at Nanga-Eboko and a gendarme introduced himself as Moses. He was very friendly and interested in my journey but not at all in the accident as he said it was not in his area, never mind that there was only one road in and one road out of the town. Another African surprise!

As Moses was friendly and appeared to be helpful, I asked if he knew a welder who could have another go at repairing the broken rear luggage frame. He took me to a welder's workshop and as the job was done a young teenager asked if he could sit on the bike and rev the engine. Foolishly I said OK and the next thing I knew he took off on the bike and disappeared down the road with everything I had, a complete nightmare of my own making. Half the town gathered around to see my distress and Moses commandeered a moped to go look for him. Just as he was about to set off in search, after ten minutes of worried waiting, there was a familiar roar and the bike came down the hill but with a different guy on it!

All seemed to be OK with both bike and luggage and I was greatly relieved and very angry with myself for having been so stupid. How lucky was I?

Eventually the culprit ambled up to me and apologised saying that he had got carried away and had wanted to show off to his pals. Moses asked if I wanted him to take any action and I said that everything was fine, no damage had been occasioned.

Out of town the track continued to be rough and potholed; the last sixty miles however were tarmacked but full of holes. As dusk settled, I swept down out of the jungle and into the Cameroonian capital.

The first task was to find a cheap hotel for the night and eventually I found one just outside the centre of town by the football stadium, called Hotel Galley. After the usual negotiations I secured a very comfortable room for just $4 per night. The room had its own en suite and the shower actually worked. One of the night staff introduced himself as Anthony and offered me any help that I might need. He was a likeable fellow and next morning helped me give Suzy a much-needed wash down in the hotel's back yard. Also, he washed my by-now-stinking nylon sleeping bag. He invited me to go with him to his house so the two of us squeezed onto the bike and spent the day playing draughts at which he was a maestro and beat me every time. His house was a shack built of mud and sticks and leant at a crazy angle with a corrugated iron roof. Inside it was very clean and tidy with mud wall and a beaten earth floor lined with carpeting. He introduced me to his family and friends and made me feel very welcome. As he had been so kind, I invited him out for an evening meal at a little restaurant of his choice and then we had a wonderful pint of Guinness at a local bar. Guinness was incredibly popular in this part of Africa, a most welcome surprise.

Monday morning I started to prepare for the next part of my trip. I changed a couple of travellers' cheques at the bank, visited the British embassy for a free letter of assistance, the Zaire embassy to arrange for a visa and the Cameroonian immigration office for an extension to my ten-day visa. That took the entire morning, and in the afternoon, I was able to purchase some eight-inch nails to use as tent pegs and also got my torn luggage bag repaired. The tourist office had little to show except for some amazing carvings and a statue of a man from the far west of the country on a horse dressed in an astonishing regalia of bright multicoloured clothing.

That afternoon with Anthony on board returning from a shopping trip to the hotel the heavens opened once more. In no time at all the streets were flooded and everything came to a standstill.

After the deluge stopped, we started back again but were soon unable to move as the red mud was so thick and sticky from the road that it totally blocked the front mudguard to the wheel, completely locking up the wheel. As I sat astride the machine, Anthony was able to scrape the thick mud out of the mudguard with a stick, but we had to repeat

Anthony and family outside their home

this operation many times on our way back to the hotel. It occurred to me that if these conditions had happened to me on some jungle road by myself, I would have been in quite a lot of trouble.

The following day was spent relaxing at the British embassy in their reading room catching up on the world's news from their newspapers, which were only two weeks old. In the afternoon Anthony took me to the city museum, which was very small and cramped with poorly labelled statues and carvings, which were very fine indeed and deserved better display. I pointed out to Anthony that there was actually more office space for the museum's officials than actual display space and wondered what they all did to keep themselves busy. Some more detailed explanations of the display items would have been good.

By now Suzy's front tyre, which was at least a year old before I left home, was beginning to look bald in a couple of areas and had certainly felt slippery and out of control when taking rough gravel corners. Following Anthony's invaluable advice I was able to locate a fairly knobbly new tyre of the right diameter and width to fit from a shop by the name of "Moto George". This shop's main exhibit was a new Yamaha XS 750cc road machine, which must have been on display for about a year. I could not help but speculate who was going to buy such a machine in Yaoundé where the roads are so bad that even to reach a speed of 30mph was to risk breaking one's neck in a pothole.

The Zaire embassy, when I went back to collect my visa, was shut for the next two days despite an assurance that my visa would be ready for collection today. This meant that I had to kick my heels in Yaoundé or could make the most of this opportunity and see a bit more of Cameroon.

So I left the city that morning and headed south and west for the 200 mile trip to the beach resort of Kribi and the Atlantic Coast. After bumping and bouncing over twenty miles of tar strip the road turned to dirt and huge clouds of choking dust would fly up as each vehicle passed. At the small town of Ebolowa approximately halfway I stopped and had a wonderful meal of roasted pig meat and large cooked bananas, which I later came to know and enjoy as plantains, very common in Central Africa.

From Ebolowa I turned westwards down a small and not so much used track to Kribi. For some unknown reason I seemed possessed by the devil and rode down that track at amazing speed, flying over crumbling wooden bridges and bouncing over potholes in the most extraordinary overconfident manner regardless of the danger to myself or of serious damage to the bike. Hitting a large pothole at speed with a grossly overloaded bike is a strange experience; one minute you are looking straight ahead trying to read the road, the next you are looking down at the front wheel from an angle of ninety degrees as my backside was violently lifted into the air by the bucking saddle. A hair-raising experience which I repeated four or five times; for some reason beyond my control I was possessed and could not make myself slow down and ride with proper care. Perhaps it was the joy of getting away from the city, or that of being alone in the jungle once more, or stranger still some sort of pygmy magic. There were pygmies there though I never saw them properly, just fleeting glimpses of small boy-like figures running away in fear from the track on hearing me coming, for they are the shy little people of the forest. This track to Kribi was 100 miles long and as a result of my speeding madness I covered it in just four hours. As the sun was setting, I reached the stunning clear blue Atlantic framed with drooping coconut palms swaying in a warm evening breeze.

As I rode around Kribi getting my bearings I came across a couple of fellow travellers, Robert and Thea from Holland. They were to repeatedly cross my path over the next two months, though I did not know that then. It was good to see them as I had not met another traveller since leaving Agadez twenty days before. After a couple of drinks and an introductory chat I left them to set off and find a bed for the night. All the cheaper-looking hotels were full so I tried for a room at the solitary rather smart one right on the beach front, which was managed by a stern German lady with whom I agreed to book a room for a couple of nights at a charge much higher than I usually paid. I had offloaded everything from the motorcycle into the room when she stormed in and demanded full immediate payment. I thought that was a real cheek so holding my ground refused to make payment, pointing out that even in Germany one pays hotel bills on departure, not on arrival. This comment only served to entrench her in her position so wearily refusing to be browbeaten I took all my luggage and strapped it back onto the bike and with no bed to go to was planning to head out to the jungle and make camp.

As I left the hotel driveway a young guy stopped me and invited me to stay at his home not far away. As he seemed OK I thought I would give it a chance so put him on board and Suzy once more had to stand the extra strain. "Very close" turned out to be a 10km ride through pitch-dark jungle following, to begin with, a much potholed dirt road, which then turned into just a footpath. Eventually we came to a steep muddy bank above his parents' fisherman's hut. I had a good look at it in the moonlight and thought that it was risky but just about feasible. So carefully I shot down the bank into the yard in front of the hut and the occupants, men, women and children rushed out of it looking completely bewildered. They insisted that the bike should not stay in the yard but quickly improvised a ramp to enable Suzy to be put in the living room! That got me a rousing clap when I completed the manoeuvre of riding up the ramp, finishing with a small collision with the dining room table.

The family were friendly enough although only the old fisherman and his son could speak French, so communication was basic and involved a lot of sign language. After a meal of fresh fish and rice, the son invited me to accompany him to the next village to show me the nightlife. We stopped at another fisherman's hut on the way where we had a couple of beers and the proprietor actually could speak a few words of pidgin English. Then we walked once more in pitch darkness on a jungle path, me slightly fearful of encountering a leopard, to a third village where there was a bar full of young girls and guys dancing the night away to African beats. In Cameroon it is not uncommon for a bar also to be a brothel with no charge for services other than the price of a drink. My companion wanted me to stay and arranged for me to dance with what he thought was the most attractive of the girls. I soon cottoned on to what it was all about and whilst still in possession of my faculties withdrew and said that I was much too tired to sleep with such a strong girl and wanted to go back to his parents' house to sleep. Dutifully my host guided me swiftly back to his hut but then asked me if I wanted to sleep with him! I told him I was not that way inclined, so he left me and went back to the village bar for his entertainment.

As soon as I got my head down, I found myself under serious attack from mosquitoes; in spite of the heat and humidity the only option was to retreat into the depths of my sleeping bag. It was a clear choice between sweating it out or being bitten to death. Eventually I dozed off fitfully on the earthen floor fearing in the back of my mind that I would not be able to get Suzy in the morning back up the earth bank to the footpath above the hut. In my nightmare it rose up to a fearsome height, but in the clear soft light of dawn I was surprised to find that I was able to tackle it fully loaded without incident.

Back in Kribi I met up once more with Robert and Thea, they kindly invited me to join them for breakfast at the house of a French guy and his Cameroonian wife whom they were staying with. Robert then showed me a reasonable hotel where they had stayed before meeting their current host. However, the bed looked as if it was infested with bed bugs as the sheets were covered with blood stains. I agreed to take the room for the next three days subject to a change of sheets and payments to be made daily. It turned out that the room was clear of bed bugs but there were as many mosquitos as in the village hut the previous night.

The rolling Atlantic provided me with some excellent swimming, and body surfing in the huge rollers was good sport; the water was pleasantly warm and not too salty. One of the most interesting local sights at Kribi was a silvery cascade of water from a river plunging down a waterfall straight into the sea in a glistening torrent. Well worth the 7km walk down the beach to reach it.

One night in my room after a couple of hours of endurance with the continual mosquito attacks there was a shy knock on the room's door. It was one of the hotel porters who had a girl who would like to sleep with me. He was quite surprised at my lack of enthusiasm; it seemed to me that promiscuity was rife in West Africa.

After a pleasant three days of R&R I got the itch to be moving on. The ride back to Yaoundé did not go well, with two punctures to my rear wheel. The first incident happened in the centre of a village and in no time I was surrounded by about thirty of its inhabitants all agog at my predicament, curious to see the repair and interested at the sight of all my tools, which I kept very close at hand in their canvas roll for fear of pilfering. After about an hour the task was completed and very kindly a girl ran up to me with a cake of soap and bowl of water for me to wash the oil and grime off my hands. One of the lads expertly lopped off the head of a coconut from a nearby tree with his panga and handed it to me to drink its sweet and refreshing milk.

Between the first and second blowouts I heard a horrible scraping noise and observed that my rear top box carrier had completely collapsed, all four supporting frame tubes having fractured once more. With a certain amount of relish, I at long last jettisoned the wretched thing and abandoned it with the five-gallon speedboat fuel container close to the roadside as no doubt it would be recycled by some future entrepreneur. This meant that I had to organise a new system of carrying my load, for the top box had provided a handy backstop to my backpack and various rolled-up items such as tent and sleeping bag, etc. Again my length of sash cord came in very handy for firmly tying the load down in a new format.

At the next village whilst repairing the second puncture a lorry rolled by and on the back a passenger proudly waved the orange five-gallon fuel container at me. At Ebolowa I bumped into Robert and Thea who had left Kribi the day before me and were staying that night in the town. After a couple of beers, I left them and found a cheap restaurant which as usual was serving meat and rice. Then I was coerced by the patron to dance with the resident tart who very soon was asking for a present. I swiftly departed into the night under a rising moon to make camp in the jungle. After 15km or so I found a road maker's clearing and set up the tent. But the ground was very rough and hard being gravel and I was disturbed by the amazing number of different noises; frogs were croaking,

Final collapse of top box frame

crickets chirruping and mystery mournful howls echoing around the surrounding jungle, which made me remember how scared the locals were of being attacked by wild animals, particularly leopards.

After a restless night I packed up at 6.30am and left in a thin mist, which added a strange tinge of blue to the jungle's predominant shade of green. This quickly cleared as the first rays of the early morning sun bit into the groove of the forest track. Just after I had got onto the narrow strip of potholed tar approaching Yaoundé and as my speed picked up, I felt the large smack of something flying into my knee. A few minutes later, a sharp stab of pain as if a red-hot needle had been inserted came from that knee causing me to holler out and swerve off the highway to a halt. As I straightened my leg out, I found an enormous black and white bee; gingerly I lifted it off my jeans and it immediately flew away. It must have been knocked out by the impact and taken its revenge when it came round.

Great news: stopping at the Zairian embassy, my visa had finally been stamped very impressively into my passport.

Back at the hotel it was good to catch up with Anthony again, also my new Dutch friends turned up in a taxi and checked into the hotel as well. I decided that it was time to go about the dirty work of changing Suzy's drive chain. The old one was by now so worn that it stretched like an old rubber band and needed constant adjustment. The three-hour job went well but in the afternoon in the town I had another rear wheel blowout and this time my tools were back at the hotel. I pushed the machine to a garage and after filling the rear tyre with air, rode like hell to get back to the hotel before the tyre was flat again, just making it.

Waves of exhaustion seemed to be plaguing me this time in Yaoundé so I decided with little persuasion necessary from Robert and Thea that I would rest up for a couple more days before travelling on. One day I was in the town when the president's motorcade was passing on his way back from the airport to the palace. I parked the bike up carefully, or so I had thought, and went to join the crowds gathering to see him pass. No sooner had I left the street where I had parked than a couple of boys ran up to me and urgently were beckoning me to return to the bike. At first, I thought that they were up to some mischief but on rounding the corner saw to my horror that the bike was lying in the gutter having been knocked over by an incompetent Renault 4 driver. As I lifted her up the police and a large crowd gathered around and the fun began. I demanded compensation there and then for a rather large dent in my fuel tank. The crowd were urging me to forgive the poor and penniless driver. The police blew their whistles and lashed out at the crowd with their battens adding to the general confusion. Finally, the driver gave me 300 CFA (about enough for a beer) then I gave him back 100 CFA and the crowd clapped their approval!

Another not so good incident also happened to me one day in town: as I walked down a busy shopping street a madman ran up to me with no warning and punched me hard in the chest. It was so quick and sudden that had he had a knife in his hand I would have been a dead man. I was completely shocked with fright but saw no reason to retaliate for the man was obviously unhinged. Contemptuously, I glared at him and crossed the street away from him; he followed me for a while and a loud stream of probably vile but incomprehensible accusations spouted from his lips.

MY WORST DAY

On the 3rd of July the hotel staff waved me off on the next stage of my journey; however, it was not to be. Seventeen miles later I had my first puncture; surrounded by a crowd of interested children I undertook the ninety-minute repair. Taking the tyre casing off I observed the cause of the many recent punctures that I had suffered. There was an ugly crack in the inner lining of the tyre and this had been pinching the inner tube to the point of puncture. I applied my largest repair patch to this crack trying to make it as smooth a bed for the inner tube to bear on as possible. Half an hour later a second puncture sent me cursing to the side of the track; this time on removing the tyre I found a leak to the new patch on the repaired inner tube. Another one and a half hours and I was mobile again. But not for long: fifty miles later the rear tyre blew out for the third time that day. I could not believe my poor luck and was beginning to feel quite despondent. After a morale-boosting banana, I set to work once more and this time discovered that the tyre now had a gaping hole on the outside of the tyre wall. I now had no option but to get back to "Moto George" at Yaoundé 120 miles back for a replacement.

In Nigeria I had had the foresight to buy for just such an emergency an aerosol can of puncture repair foam. Carefully following the can's instructions in no time at all the tyre was firmly inflated.

Twenty miles back down the track a village policeman ordered me to halt. After looking at my passport and other documents he declared that the place where I had entered Cameroon did not exist in spite of the stamps confirming my entry point had been Boukoala. He said that this stamp must be forged; a cold shiver ran down my spine when he predictably went on to insist that I must be a spy!

What other motive possibly could I have for riding a motorcycle across Cameroon? As by now he had pocketed my passport, there appeared to be very little that I could do but politely contest his allegations. We spent two hours at the village checkpoint surrounded by a large crowd of locals all come to gawp at the white spy and the power that their own policeman had over him. Now and then a truck would trundle through the village and on each occasion this little Hitler would rush out and attempt to stop the vehicle. More often than not though they would ignore him and keep on going much to the amusement of the onlooking villagers, who would clap and cheer on each occasion. I believe that his reputation was well known.

I asked him why these vehicles did not stop for him as after all he carried a gun; surely he could shoot them if they did not stop. Ruefully he said that he was forbidden to shoot in this situation and anyway had no bullets. He then asked me to follow him in a pickup that he had managed to commandeer back to his police station 25km away down the track. At the police station were a couple of his superiors one of whom appeared to be drunk and a nasty piece of work.

They started the interrogation immediately, their eyes flashing angrily as they loudly and repeatedly shouted at me, "You are a spy," "Your passport is forged," "Which airport did you land at?"

All of them refused to believe that I was an innocent tourist and insisted that I must have some ulterior motive for travelling across Africa on a motorcycle. Whenever I got impatient with these childish accusations, they added insult to injury by threatening to put me in their cell, which already contained two probably innocent inmates.

However, they relented on that threat but then decided to put me in the spare cell whilst they decided what they were going to do with me. There was no chance of me contacting the British embassy from here as the station had no phone or even a radio, so I knew I was on my own and would have to use all my diplomacy and wits to see me through; above all I told myself to remain calm and polite.

Eventually after another two hours they pulled me out and started another session of relentless questioning. Then the lead interrogator, possibly sobering up, wrote a long report in his notebook and asked me to sign it at the bottom. I agreed to do this but added to the report to say that I was a tourist riding across Cameroon and could not understand a word of the French report that I had signed.

It was sundown when they eventually released me, but there was no way I was going to hang around anywhere near that police station. Shaking the dust off my boots so to speak I rode out of that village and away once more Yaoundé bound. I nearly cried when the final act of bad luck occurred; in darkness travelling down a steep incline with jungle either side I had the fourth blowout of the day!

There was some cleared flat ground close by so I pitched my tent with the help of a delightful old man who stopped to see if I was OK and decided that the repair would have to wait for the sunup on the morrow. Just before I turned in, a happy passing drunk gave me a swig of some revolting banana beer as a nightcap, real jungle juice. When I emerged from my tent the old man who had helped me with the tent the night before drove by and stopped again to see if I had had a good night. Refreshed, with faith once more restored in humanity, I undertook my repair, which amazingly held good all the way this time until I reached "Moto George".

The only tyre they had suitable for the wheel was the same as the one that I had purchase for the front wheel the week before. Although it was 5cm narrower than the correct width, it worked and indeed lasted all the way to Tanzania.

At the Hotel Galley everyone was amazed to see me back once more. All afternoon I slept in exhaustion and on rising joined Robert and Thea for a grilled fish supper in their room bought from street vendors – delicious. After this we went a bit crazy and joined the Saturday night party in the hotel's dining room, which had been converted into a disco for the evening. The dancing was fantastic to watch and we all ended up drinking far too much; as a consequence my head was pounding the next morning.

In spite of not feeling well I took a couple of aspirin, loaded up and once more said farewell to all with many a joke about returning again in a couple of days – Hotel California! Yaoundé had been a very enjoyable city for me, though destiny seemed to make it hard to leave.

The ride was pretty uneventful this time, the small narrow rear tyre was slippery taking corners on the tarmac but firmed up on the dirt track. People waved as I passed, but it was far too risky to wave back. I passed a severely jackknifed wreck, a reminder of how bad the local driving standards could be. Perhaps this driver had tried to wave back?

Mud clogged up the wheels at one point causing great loss of power and engine overheating. I stopped and it took me ten minutes to clear the mud clogging the mudguards both front and rear; it was only three minutes later that it was caked up again.

We made the border post after thirty hours of travel and crossed at the post at Bertoua, with few hassles, into the Central African Republic.

Chapter 11

CENTRAL AFRICAN REPUBLIC

THE TRACK DETERIORATED AGAIN NEAR TO BOAUR, BUT THE SCENERY WAS delightful with lovely views and no jungle to block them; many small villages clung to the route. In the late afternoon Suzy developed a puncture in the middle of Boaur's crossroads. Kids sprang up from nowhere and helped me push the bike out of the road and into the shady porch of a nearby guest house where I took a small room with no electric light but a hurricane lamp in lieu. That evening I went out to explore the town and called in at an obviously popular bar crowded with happy faces. I was immediately offered a seat in the busy room and a beer. Locals here buy one large bottle of beer per table and share it around the table whilst it is still cool so it does not end up getting warm in the glass, a great idea and a very sociable way to drink. An attractive girl asked me where I was staying but I suspected that the question was made with ulterior motive and declined to answer. Feeling hungry I went out and outside the bar found a line of women selling all sorts of street food; they sold me some fried doughnuts and hot pimento and meat soup.

On the way out of town I passed a couple of jeeps crewed by some white French foreign legionnaires brandishing weapons, a strange sight I had not been expecting to encounter in this remote part of the world. Again, later on the jungle track I came around a bend and nearly collided with a French army patrol of armoured cars going the other way; probably they had a base nearby and were conducting routine patrols.

Then the skies opened and I had to stop and take cover under a bush for an hour or so; when I resumed the journey the track had turned into a riverbed with mud, pebbles, sand and rock all swept into piles in disarray. Large channels of flowing water had to be crossed with care where they flowed across the track at each point of watershed. Speed was reduced to below 20mph over the next fifty miles and in many villages the going became even more difficult for the road surface was always much worse with deeper and more frequent potholes and ruts, probably due to the increase in traffic or else deliberately left in a poor state to reduce traffic speed through the village.

In villages also I had learnt that one always had to be wary of the chickens who were invariably suicidal; they would be determined to cross from the safe far side of the road to the dangerous motorcycle side in an instant which cost four of them their lives over the next few weeks. Pigs would hold their ground in determined fashion and then deliberately cross just in front with a malicious squeal of delight. Goats were much nimbler and more considerate. I shall never forget one heart-stopping moment of seemingly inevitable collision with a plump sow who aggressively crossed the road to get at me. I was so startled I plunged straight over three potholes in a row to get away from her. Needless to say, ten minutes later I was cursing about another puncture. By the evening I arrived at the town of Bossentele, a crossroads town memorable to me not for the small hut I was able to hire for the night but for the huge thunderclouds alive with lighting strikes and behind them a large moon was just visible above the horizon. A strange phenomenon, particularly because the thunderclaps were too far away to be audible.

The capital city of Bangui was just an easy six-hour morning's ride 270 miles from here on a newly laid and smooth tar highway, oh the joy and the difference a good tar road can provide. Just outside the city was an immigration checkpoint; the officials were friendly and helpful, one of them wanted to buy my machine and offered 300,000 CFA (about £1000). A very good offer and I did consider it but concluded that no matter how much I was offered the challenge of riding through Africa was worth more to me than money.

Bangui proved to be a pleasant town on the banks of the wide Ubangi river with French colonial-style buildings and shady tree-lined boulevards. Zaire was visible across the river with wild jungle-clad hills awaiting my discovery.

In the market I bumped into a Dane who said that he had just crossed over the river from Zaire with his Land Rover now only running in fourth gear; we arranged to meet up later for a beer and for me to buy his surplus unused Zaire money with my surplus CFAs. He had some very interesting tales of his trip up through Zaire, how the ferries had to be seen to be believed and how at one stage they had to make their own road north of Kisangani. Petrol, he assured me, was generally unobtainable except at the odd mission station or else from one or other of the jungle logging companies.

For the first night I secured a rather grand room in a decaying colonial hotel stinking of blocked drain, which I was tired enough to ignore. As soon as dusk fell the streets of Bangui emptied and everything closed up, most unlike any other African cities, which very much were full of life at night. Perhaps it was a throwback to the despotic and murderous days of Emperor President Bokassa and his curfew. He had only been deposed two years before my trip.

Next morning, I discovered one of Bangui's famed delights, beautiful crisp fresh French baguettes, mouth-watering and bizarrely available in the very heart of Africa. An issue for me to resolve was to find a good and cheap place to stay for the next few days to rest and bring Suzy up to scratch for the most difficult remaining 2000km plus stretch of my journey across the vast Congo forests and on down to Tanzania. Eventually just out of the city I found a place called "Le Centre Protestant pour les Jeunes" where a bed in a shared dormitory was available for just £1 per night. Coincidentally it turned out to be quite a travellers' sanctuary, with most of the dormitory's occupants being overlanders. As my various bags were brought in one after the other, guests crowded around and openly speculated about my mode of transport. Obviously, no hitchhiker could travel so laden. There was general amazement when I explained that I was travelling on a six-year-old road motorcycle which was parked just outside.

An interesting character of this lodging was a young long-haired Canadian from trappers' country North of Quebec. This lad, Michell, only twenty-one years old, had over the past three months ridden a second-hand bicycle from Ouagadougou in Upper Volta, across Ghana, Togo, Nigeria and Cameroon to the Central African Republic. Outside Bouar his luck had run out and he had collapsed by the roadside with what later proved to be hepatitis, a common scourge afflicting many travellers in central Africa. A passing missionary found him and took him to the mission station where he spent the next two weeks in recovery. He followed the advice given that he should sell the bicycle and return home to recover; however, a week after he sold the bike he felt well enough to continue his trip, but regretfully with no bicycle.

Another character was a Frenchman called Alain who was working in Banui as a sales representative for a bookselling company. Every morning without fail on waking he would roll a large joint of local grass before even lifting his mosquito net. He had a very battered old Peugeot which he had driven down to here from France following almost the same route as myself.

Also in the dormitory were a German couple called Pepi and Lala; they were brother and sister and Pepi had spent the last two years travelling all over Africa. On his map was a redline showing the route that he had taken, which looked like a red piece of spaghetti zigzagging up every other highway and byway. Lala had flown in three or four months earlier to join in for the last year of his trip.

As we were all gelling very well with each other we decided to live as a commune, so Michell and I were delegated to go to the market to buy food for all for that evening. The city market was large and rich with local produce all beautifully displayed; it was spotless with individual pieces of fruit or vegetables glistening with drops of water splashed on to keep them fresh and cool. Bargaining was fast and furious; it took us a good hour and a half to purchase the goods necessary for dinner and breakfast the following day on good terms. Our last purchase had been a large pineapple from which Michell tore the green head off and finding nowhere to dispose of it placed it in the gutter. No sooner had his hand disconnected with it when a large Market Mama screamed abuse at us and rushing forward picked it up and placed it back in a rather startled Michell's hand.

As supper was under preparation on an odd assortment of gas and petrol cookers in the dormitory, Robert and Thea, my Dutch friends last seen in Yaoundé, appeared, tired, hungry but delighted to meet up again.

Back in town next day I went hunting for some replacement wheel spokes as a couple of mine had broken, causing minor distortion of the wheel and additional wobble more noticeable on tar at speed than on a dirt track. I was very pleased to find some new ones which, although were for a Peugeot Mobylette, were of the same length as Suzy's and they screwed into position, tightened up and strengthened the wheel adequately.

The next nine days passed in a blur of eating, sleeping, card-playing and just enjoying the company and camaraderie of my fellow travellers. Looking back on my trip, that time in Bangui stands out as a very pleasant highlight of the trip. The close feeling of unity, fellowship and shared experience was very enriching; I had never lived in a community before or since and it was a wonderful time for me, a solo traveller.

Every night a sumptuous communal meal was prepared from the finest produce and goodies that Bangui market could offer, except for monkey meat, which we drew a line at. Firm favourite as chef was Michell; he was unsurpassed for the fine quality of his fried plantains. After eating, some of us would then head out to the bars of what was known as Kilometre 5; as mentioned before the city centre was completely dead at night but out in this location the lights were on all and every night. Bar after bar pounded out Afro-Rock and Zairean music in a competing cacophony of sound. Beer was 20p a bottle and all the bars had dance floors alive with happy faces, white teeth flashing in the spotlights. Michell with his long hair was often mobbed by the girls; often even when out in the town in the day they would run up to him, just to touch and stroke his hair.

Michell (hair tied back) at the Ubangi River waiting for the ferry to Zaire

Another day I was shopping in town with Robert and Thea when some giggling girls rushed up to us from behind and stroked our arms and then ran away; it was a bit disconcerting at first but we soon learnt to accept it as some sort of showing-off game.

A week after arriving in Bangui we heard a rumour that there had been a bomb explosion in the town's cinema and that three people had been killed; supporters of the recently deposed President Bokassa were thought to be responsible in protest at the French-led and successful coup of 1979. Many of the local people we spoke to expressed support for him as they viewed him as a "strong" leader.

However, he was a despot who bankrupted the country with a most elaborate and unnecessary plan to form the first empire in Africa and spent an estimated $20 million on his coronation in an attempt to copy the coronation of Napoleon I as Emperor of the French in 1804. No world leaders attended the ceremony despite many lavish invitations, and he was viewed to be insane by many.

Although he was an embarrassment to the French, who had originally supported his coup back in 1965, he was for many years tolerated and supplied with arms and aid due to the coveted uranium deposits at Bakwoma, big game hunting grounds near the Sudanese border and diamonds, both of which President Giscard d'Estaing of France became very partial to; this resulted in a scandal known as the "Diamonds Affair" and ultimately contributed to his downfall from the French presidency.

By January 1979, French support for Bokassa had all but eroded after food riots in Bangui led to a massacre of civilians. The final straw came between 17th April and 19th April, when a large number of elementary school students in Bangui and elsewhere in the country were arrested after they had protested against paying for and wearing the expensive government-required school uniforms with Bokassa's image on them. Around a hundred children were killed. Bokassa allegedly participated in the massacre, appearing at the jail and beating some of the children to death with his cane.

The massive worldwide press coverage which followed the deaths of the students opened the way for a successful coup, which saw French troops invade the Central African Empire and restore former President David Dacko to power, while Bokassa fled into exile by aeroplane in September 1979.

The day after the cinema bomb in Bangui, a large white GB-registered Bedford truck marked "Guerba Expeditions" with a group of overlanders on board pulled into our hostel. They had earlier that day tried to cross the Ubangi river by ferry but it turned out that the border was shut due to the bomb outrage. Most of the dormitory travellers who were going south were now decided to cross over the river to Zaire as soon as possible and so the following day we spent the whole day waiting down at the ferry point for the border to open, but it was a non-event.

After a three-hour wait the following morning the ferry and border post at last was in operation.

Chapter 12

ZAIRE

THE FERRY SAILED QUICKLY ACROSS THE UBANGI IN TEN MINUTES AND DEPOSITED us all at the village of Zongo where it seemed as if the entire village had come down to the waterside to meet the ferry and the Zaire immigration and customs post officials were waiting, keen for work after the three-day border closure. They insisted in being as bureaucratic as possible and wanted to count all foreign currency and travellers' cheques, etc. They decided in front of everyone to search me for undeclared money and asked me to turn out my pockets. They found 1500 CFA undeclared in my wallet but not the £10 note in my shirt pocket concealed in a letter nor the £100 sitting in my underpants! To be fair I was expecting them to confiscate the CFAs they had found, but no, they insisted in changing it into Zairian money but at the poor official rate of exchange.

At last we were able to proceed and accompanying the truck we headed south-west down a sandy track so little used that vegetation was growing down its centre. The truck just plodded along at 20mph which was way slower than the 30mph I could comfortably achieve. So I pushed on ahead alone and waited at the next crossroads for them to catch up.

By dusk we had passed through the settlement of Libenge and pressed on through in the gathering gloom down a track until we found an abandoned hut which had a clearing in front where we could pitch our camp. It was a great event for the occupants of the other nearby huts who gathered around as spellbound children to watch the strange sight of a dozen white people erecting tents and then cooking supper. They kindly gave us pineapples and nuts and we gave them cigarettes and entertainment. I joined the tour group's supper of tomato soup, liver and onions with rice, sitting on chairs and at a table produced from

Bow and arrow guard for the washer women deep in the forest of Zaire

the depths of the Bedford; these fellows really travelled in style. Apparently, they even had a shower.

We tried to find out from the villagers if the bridge further on was still in use as we had not met a single vehicle coming in the opposite direction, but no one seemed to know or care. I left the camp a few minutes before the truck and three miles further on reached the bridge. It was looking very sick indeed, sagging on one side at an angle of thirty degrees to horizontal. Otherwise it was typical of many African jungle river bridges, two large tree trunks laid across the span with a couple of timber piers on each side. On top of the two tree trunk beams was a latticework of smaller timbers running perpendicular across and finally two lengths of planks formed a running track for vehicle wheels to follow for the full length of the bridge. Half of this bridge had collapsed because one side of the support piers had been washed away in the rains a few days before.

After a brief inspection I cautiously rode Suzy across, looking neither left nor right but dead ahead focussed on the line of the track beyond the bridge end. I was shaking when I got across and stopped for a cigarette and to watch how the Bedford would manage. Just as I was turning the bike around to watch more comfortably from the saddle I suddenly

Typical jungle track bridge

felt her going backwards over the road edge towards the river below. With no time to think I instinctively snatched her forward, rear wheel spinning as it chewed its way back up onto the track. A very close call indeed, only just avoiding complete disaster.

Before I had time to get underneath the bridge to have a closer examination of the piers, the truck arrived and I warned Bob the driver that it would be a bit touch and go for them. We had a quick cursory look underneath and Bob said he was going to have a crack at getting across; he made all his passengers cross the bridge ahead of him on foot then very gingerly set out alone at the wheel. A murmur of relief and a loud creak from the bridge greeted the moment when the rear wheels reached the track. Poor Bob was drowning in perspiration.

A few miles further down the jungle track I came across a lorry lying on its side by the bank of the track. A huge jungle creeper had been tied to the side of the vehicle with which the driver and passengers had made several failed attempts to pull it upright. They told me that the accident had happened last night but fortunately nobody had been hurt. I continued on my way and soon reached the banks of a wide and slow-flowing muddy river. Bob later told me he was able, using the Bedford, to right the vehicle for them.

There was a concrete slipway leading down steeply to the water's edge and at its end to one side lay the remains of a half sunken and rusty iron barge, which looked as if it had been last used several years before. However, there were no other boats in sight, bar some pirogues, and a local assured me that yes, this was the ferry. I asked in my faltering French where the captain was, only to learn that he was at lunch. One or two enterprising locals paddled up in their pirogues and asked to be allowed to take me across; it really was amusing to explain that it would not be possible, for how could the bike fit inside a pirogue, and even if it did, it would probably capsize.

An old man walked down to me on the causeway and beckoned me to follow him up the track. To my complete surprise a large white wicker armchair had been placed in the welcome shade of a palm tree in the middle of the road. I began to feel as if I was a colonial official on some important mission in the Victorian era. A few minutes later as the truck arrived around the bend in the road everyone hooted with mirth at the unexpected sight; all that was missing was a topee.

After a while the ferry lads emerged from the village and began to bail out the rusting sunken craft.

In around half an hour the ferry was in position and floating at the bottom of the slipway and I was waved on as first to load. No simple task, for the loading ramp was inoperative being seized in a position a couple of feet above the craft's decking. A ramp was made from a few planks to go from the slipway to the craft and with some difficulty I rode down the slipway and over the ramp, applying my brakes as we landed in the craft and skidding on a large patch of oil much to the general entertainment of all. The big white Bedford boarded the ferry without too much trouble and then also a third smaller truck. The ferry was powered by diesel fuel taken from the trucks and started using jump leads from them as well. As the old engine started it let out a huge bang and a cloud of diesel smoke obscured all views and then we were off on our way but with seemingly no operative steering as we spun around 360 degree circles at least four times before colliding with the opposite bank!

I was first to disembark, edging with some trepidation down a narrow plank and through several feet of river water to reach dry land without incident. Although the bike's ignition points must have been submerged, she did not falter. The overlanders' truck likewise came off with no incident; however, in the manoeuvre the ferry got pushed further out into the deeper water of the river. This meant that the third truck's front wheels plunged down into the water leaving its rear wheels spinning in the water as its tail was caught on the ferry's defective loading ramp. This tricky predicament was solved by the Bedford attaching a tow rope to the trapped vehicle and pulling it off the ferry and up the riverbank.

Guerba Expedition Bedford about to offload from ferry

Bailed-out ferry with inoperative ramp and no steering!

Saying goodbye to my friendly group of overlanders I set off ahead for the jungle town of Gemena where I was able to refuel completely at the town's cotton depot. There was a beautiful church by the town's mission and I called in to get advice on where to stay and to gather the latest news. However, the Belgian priest was very unfriendly and I suspected slightly batty; he told me that I could not stay there even before I had asked and that he wanted me to go away. Somewhat abashed, I took refuge at the house next door where a contrastingly friendly man resided. He allowed me to put up my tent at the bottom of his garden right next door to the mission church and sent his house watchman to guard me all night armed with a bow and arrow! Some village boys gathered around out of curiosity, but he shooed them away. However, I went out in the road to ask them if they could buy me something to eat as I was down to my last can of sardines. A few minutes later one of them returned with a strange-looking root tuber which I knew to be cassava. I did not have much of a clue what to do with it so asked my night watchman to advise. Taking my Swiss Army penknife he cut off the skin and sliced thin slivers for me to eat. Its flavour was none too bad but with a slight aroma similar to turpentine, so assisted by hunger, I managed to eat half of the root mixed with my sardines.

As I broke camp the Guerba Expedition truck pulled up and once more we exchanged news and greetings. I decided to stay behind because I wanted to experience an African Mass in the church, it being Sunday. I had heard the female choristers practising the night before and it sounded fantastic.

It was indeed a glorious and spectacular event; the church was spilling over with worshippers and the service was sung entirely by the choir with the priest swaying from side to side with each hymn's rhythm and the whole congregation dancing together as one. The service took two hours to finish and I was completely spellbound by the joy and vivacity of the experience.

I fell twice on the lonely sandy track heading east for Businga, on which giant puddles had formed that had crater-like edges of sand which had to be carefully skirted around. That second fall was bad as I was trapped under the machine for about two minutes as I had failed to sidestep off quickly enough as the bike went down. With leaking petrol spraying onto the hot engine, I gave my all to struggle free, shaking in fright. Around a bend a few minutes later I met Paul and Phillipe, two French bike riders on rugged scrambler machines who were on their way up from Rwanda. We stopped, shared cigarettes and chatted for a while, exchanging news, the roads ahead and recommendations of places to stay, etc. One never knows who you are going to meet around the next bend in Africa!

At around 4pm I arrived at the banks of the Mongala river, a wide tributary of the Congo river. Overall an enjoyable ride, despite the falls, of some 100 miles taking about five hours. On my side of the bank was the port of Akula, a dirty and squalid place. As I went down to the ferry, I was greeted by the sight of my old friends in the white Guerba Bedford as they were scrambling up the far riverbank. I had hoped to catch up with them for dinner that night.

The dirty atmosphere of Akula coupled with warnings of "les voleurs" was not conducive to an overnight stay but with dusk falling I knew that the ferry would not be crossing again until the next day. At sundown, the river itself was beautiful, flowing gently, and every so often a virtual floating garden of river weeds drifted past. My meditation was interrupted by the shout from a passing pirogue elegantly streamlined in the pathway of the setting sun offering to take myself and Suzy over the water. Once more I had to point out the impossibility of the proposal.

After sundown I rode back the way I had come for a few kilometres looking for a safe place for the night. At a village I was kindly offered shelter and a bed for the night in a hut, which I gratefully accepted, but the mosquitos were terrible resulting in a sleepless night of bombardment despite my invaluable mosquito net being put to use. The morning coffee was great.

Back at Akula when I arrived early for the first ferry a large crowd of people had gathered surrounding an absolutely terrified thief who was tightly bound up with jungle creepers. The police had caught him in the night stealing coffee sacks from a nearby boat. He was with three others who all jumped into the waters to escape but this man could not swim. His eyes were full of doleful defeat.

The ferry was now back on my side of the river and after brewing myself a quick cup of tea it was time to board. Dismounted, I drove the bike into the river in first gear, riding her on the clutch. The front wheel of the bike dipped down into the river and then emerged climbing the boarding plank, but the rear one spun when it hit the plank and we were only saved by a quick-thinking bystander who rushed into the river to help me push the machine up the plank.

On from the river I continued to follow the Bedford's tyre tracks from the previous day laid down in the sandy track, which was very deteriorated in places, and I was not helped by the onset of rain and as the heavens opened the track quickly became a swift-flowing river. Deciding to press on slowly rather than halting and risking not being able to restart the engine due to dampness around the open suppressor caps on the ageing ignition leads, I soon found out that it was no longer possible to detect the potholes through the flowing brown mud. At one point I entered what on the surface looked like a normal 15ft puddle and sunk down in it, submerging the engine to close to knee height, but amazingly, she took it in her stride and pulled through it. But a few minutes later I entered another puddle with not such fortunate results. Down we went into this innocent-looking puddle, which turned out to be deep and lined with thick squidgy mud. Suzy sank until the lower engine block and frame were sucked under; as I dismounted, she was balancing upright by herself!

Luck once more was on my side for the incident happened right outside a village hut and the inhabitants willingly ran out in the rain to assist with the extraction; heaving and panting, we pushed the machine to a dryer spot. I rested a while, waiting for a break in the rain, before continuing on my way only to slither wildly out of control down a steep and muddy hill falling over at the bottom in a rut just in front of an old man. He helped me up and asked me in faltering French if I was a priest!

I could only assume that he thought that all white men in these parts were priests, for he most earnestly told me of his faith confirmed by his burning old rheumy eyes and would have nothing to do with my protestations that I was not what he thought.

I scrambled up the other equally steep side of the hill and close to the top got bogged down once more in sand, causing one spark plug to give up the ghost. Some children on seeing me ran down the hill and helped me push the bike up the remaining climb to the hilltop, for which I rewarded them with some sweets from my front tank haversack.

By 4pm I arrived in the missionary town of Lisala on the banks of the mighty Congo absolutely wacked after a very tough ride of about 100 miles over ten hours. The mission station was a grand old colonial building located high above the river affording spectacular views across and then on over mile after mile of green-topped jungle. A boy ran out of the mission on my arrival, sent down from the building with the news that Robert and Thea were staying there; it was a nice feeling to be finding more old friends again. A very friendly Father Lea greeted us with nice cold beer and showed us all to a couple of guest rooms that the mission could provide. He apologised for the lack of bed linen and lighting as they had been stolen and in consequence, they no longer felt able to charge guests for the use of the rooms but would welcome a donation in lieu. There I had the luxury of my first wash since leaving Bangui four days ago, using a large bucket of cold water borrowed from the mission's garage; so nice to feel fresh and clean once more.

Lisala turned out to be quite an attractive town high on top of a 300ft hill with great views over the two-mile-wide river. The far bank was fringed with a seemingly endless and impenetrable tangle of green jungle. At the bank they said that I could not change any travellers' cheques but after persuasion agreed to radio the HQ in Kinshasa for permission. When we returned later in the afternoon, they had not had a reply and had no idea of the rate of exchange. This was a big problem, for Robert, Thea and myself had all decided that it would be a fantastic experience to buy tickets to travel down the Congo river by ferry/barge to Kisangani some 600km away, and we did not have sufficient money to buy the tickets without changing some travellers' cheques. Ferries only departed south approximately once every ten days or so and we did not want to miss the departure of the next boat.

We decided to give up on the bank and instead resort to a black market currency exchange service. Sure enough after asking around back at the mission a Belgian father had a friend who could sometimes help travellers in need.

In the afternoon a delightful old lady appeared with a basket on her head full of ripe guavas; they were nice, sweet and cheap so we gorged ourselves to lift our spirits. In the evening Robert and I went down to the city market to discover that onions were costing $1 each, all the more reason to change money on the black market quickly. We were also surrounded by people trying to sell us large juicy caterpillars, some brown and others green and squiggly in their bowls. Others had been fried, slotted on the end of a stick and coated in crispy batter.

At the following midday, one of the missionary fathers' friends drove us in his jeep to the house of his Portuguese trader friend. After much talk over tea about the difficulties of exchanging money in the town, probably a ploy to up his profit, we agreed on a rate and amount to be exchanged.

Suddenly his houseboy pointed down to the river from the veranda at a large boat arriving at the port below. This took us by surprise as we had not been expecting our boat for a couple more days; we bid a hasty farewell to our black market friend and raced off down to the docks to buy tickets and then back up to the mission to be met halfway by the rush of townsfolk heading down to the dock for the big event of the week, the boat being the city's only real contact with the outside world.

At the mission we madly packed everything up in fair disorder and I rode down to the now crowded dock with one hand on the handlebars and the other holding onto a bag I had not had time to tie on.

At first, I panicked at the close sight of the ferry, there being seemingly no way of getting Suzy up to the decks high above the dockside mooring barge. The ferry consisted of two huge double-storey barges tied together with ropes and shunted by a third tug-like boat. Only the front first barge was moored to the mooring barge adjacent to the quayside. It was also immediately apparent that there was no communication between the shore and the captain's bridge on the rear tug and that consequently the bike-loading operation would have to be attempted knowing that at any time the captain could decide just to cast off. Robert and Thea knowing of my dilemma even offered to stay behind in the hope that the next ferry might be more suitable for loading, a kind offer which I would not hear of but which touched me deeply. I decided come hell or high water to take my chance as best I could. The first issue was to get Suzy down onto the curved hatch of the mooring barge some 3ft below the level of the quay. Looking around I spotted two curved steel struts and these I manoeuvred together to form a ramp down to the mooring barge hatch covers. Dripping with perspiration from the effort I edged the bike down the ramp and braked to a halt on the apex of the curved hatch cover. The next issue was to raise the bike up onto the deck of the front prow of the lead ferry barge, another 3ft above. Some people from the now crowded boat placed a plank from the ferry over the gap to where I was on the hatch covers. Once more I revved Suzy up and shot up the plank waggling past a couple of mooring buoys and landed on the front deck of the barge to general applause.

I was shaking with relief from the exertion, but hugely exhilarated to have achieved the loading with no loss or injury. I waved to Robert and Thea who then came aboard, and we shared a cigarette in relief together. A few minutes later the ship's ropes were cast off and we were on our way up the Congo without a hoot or any warning at all of departure.

Robert and bike on the ferry from Lisala to Kisangani

No sooner had we cast off than a dozen women came up to us bearing beautiful woven baskets of salted fish on their heads and started to surround the deck around Suzy with the fish to dry them out in the sun. It was all I could do to prevent them from draping them all over the bike as well. The stench of drying fish was overpowering and became very familiar over the next few days as there was nowhere on board to escape it.

It was a nice feeling to be moving once more and for about the first time on the trip I could relax and enjoy the scenery; whilst the boat did all the work, the world slid by. The ship's purser and crew were very friendly and cleaned out a cabin for us; on the top deck of our barge we soon discovered a bar which sold fantastic cold "Primus" beer. Not so fantastic though was our first meal that afternoon, rice and beans protein enhanced by weevils and cockroaches, which was not what we had envisaged when we paid the extra amount for our tickets to have our meals included, and so we told the purser, who pretended not to understand. Eventually he agreed though to supply us with coffee, bread and margarine instead. The bar above our cabin became alive with passengers dancing in exotic rhythm to the endless blaring of Zairian steel band music from a powerful speaker at full volume. Soon we had made many friends and begun to feel comfortable and at home.

The dawn was pink and clouded by river haze, which then lifted at sunrise. We passed many small fishing settlements on the banks and plenty of luxuriously thick jungle falling to the water but no wild animals on shore. There must have been hundreds of hippos and crocodiles but even using my field glasses it was difficult to distinguish a log from a croc on the far banks over a kilometre away. Robert claimed to see the first croc. By mid-afternoon, the stench of drying fish was really getting to us and the fish had been joined by a couple of skinned monkeys tied to a pole and almost looking as small humans crawling with maggots. We retreated to the bar; however, the music blaring out was too loud to allow for conversation, which was only possible by shouting in each other's ears. A friendly Zairian soldier we had been talking to the night before lurched over to us half drunk and offered some whisky. It was incredibly strong fire water, whatever it was, which seared my moderately seasoned throat and set me spluttering to the amusement of all. By evening our soldier friend was lying in a dead stupor having drunk himself under the table. A couple of his fellow comrades picked him up by his arms and his belt and took him away to his bed. The bar was full of people dancing the night away; they danced in an unusual manner, just shuffling their feet, totally caught in the rhythm of the music, with eyes glazed with gratification. At midnight the boat docked at a large village and the loudspeakers were turned outwards to face the mooring barge which became a huge dance floor for the hundreds of people who had come down from the village. Absolutely enthralling to watch.

After hearing how common it was for these ferry barges to plough into sand banks at night, I chained Suzy using my padlock and cables to the barge's winch post, there being little if anything to stop her sliding off the deck in the event of impact.

We learnt that many of the barge passengers were actually traders and the barge also operated as a floating market. During the day every other cabin would operate as a shop with displays of cigarettes, perfume, tinned fish, margarine, beads, shells, bangles and many other goods. As we passed the many fisherfolks' villages they would rush out in their pirogues to intercept the barges. Their dugouts would be piled high with fresh produce, fish, turtles, jungle fruits and vegetables, which they would barter to the onboard traders and passengers.

The ferry barges were going full speed upriver, which could make the tying up alongside and boarding from a pirogue really quite hazardous. Landing was also not helped by the established practice of the traders throwing rags into the pirogue to reserve first negotiating rights just at the critical moment of docking. Many a time I witnessed the procedure go wrong, the pirogue turning 180 degrees in the water and several black heads bobbing up and down in the ship's wake and the riverbank a great distance away. Many must have been drowned or eaten by crocodiles, no attempt at rescue was ever made.

However, it was fascinating to watch the skill with which these brave river folks danced their frail narrow crafts around this river queen; each would be attached by a long length of jungle creeper and some of the later arrivals were tied in alongside in rows of up to seven canoes.

In the morning of our third day on board the terrain of the riverbanks changed to high sandstone cliffs capped with the evergreen of the unending jungle. The early morning pirogues brought in supplies of fresh pineapple and avocadoes. We purchase he largest pineapple I have ever seen for about 20p, a monster weighing in at about 3kg. Our lazy journey continued on in relaxed mode of beers, card games, poker dice and snoozing in the afternoon's heat and plenty of dripping chunks of our beautifully sweet and juicy pineapple as refreshment.

We were greeted on the following morning's arrival at Kisangani by a loud pealing of church bells from the town's elegant cathedral, a veritable Notre Dame. At the docks we swiftly unloaded all our bags and a few dock hands gave me assistance in pushing the bike off the greasy barge deck and up a very steeply inclined passenger walkway to the quay. Just as I had completed strapping my bags back on to the bike an immigration officer summoned us all to his office. We were asked a persistent stream of questions but were given no time to answer before the next torrent of enquiry spewed out from his lips. After giving him a few anti-malarial pills and a couple of pencils, however,

Pirogue traders tying up to ferry in transit

he calmed down a bit. There was a nasty moment for me when he asked me to show my foreign currency for him to check against the declared sum on my entry form, for I had been playing the black market all the way. Somehow I managed to pull out the exact correct amount from a plastic bag concealing with my hand half of the notes that should not have been there.

After an hour we were cleared to leave the docks and headed for the Hotel Olympia which we had been recommended to stay at by other travellers; it was a nice place and a real travellers' haunt. I got consent to camp in the hotel's front garden for a small fee and Robert and Thea got a room to themselves. We met many other travellers there whom we had not seen before and it was good to socialise in a wider crowd. Close to the hotel was Kisangani market, a large colourful affair full of fruit, meat and vegetable stalls spread over a vast area. The next issue was to source the black market again; after asking around I was advised to go and see the Administrative Pere of the Catholic missions. He gave a very good rate of exchange, so I gave him a wad of zaires back for the mission fund.

Kisangani was a nice resting point but after a few days I realised that there was little of interest for me in the town and not a lot else to do other than eat, drink and socialise, so I set about making leaving preparations once more. The next stage of my route lay north, then east and south on a 400-mile circuitous route to Beni, the next place where fuel supplies could be assured. This route to Beni was pretty much the only one left in operation out of what had been the Belgian Congo. I tried to get assurances from the Mission HQ in town that the missions on route might be able to supply me with petrol, but to no avail. I would just have to take my chance.

That evening after dark there was the most amazing storm; as I bolted from my tent to the safety of the hotel building a sizzling bolt of lightning flashed past my ear with a whack and then an ear-splitting crash made me jump out of my skin as the strong aroma of burnt electrical discharge hit my nostrils. The sky was wonderful to look at with zigzag flashes of lightning seemingly stretching from horizon to horizon.

After a very pleasant few days' R&R I said a fond farewell to Robert and Thea and loaded up Suzy once more and rode out of town on a newly tarred and smooth highway, so nice I missed my turn-off by five miles and had to backtrack to find it, annoying for I felt the need to be conserving my fuel. The dirt road from the turn-off was so good I was able to hit 50mph and fifth gear for some stretches, but always had to be alert for potholes. The jungle got denser and more closed in around and over the track; by mid-afternoon I had arrived at my goal for the day, the small town of Bafwasende, and a friendly policeman told me by chance that there was a lorry in town with petrol on board. Suzy needed just twelve litres to fill her up, which was pretty good as we had travelled 263km from Kisangani that day.

By dusk I had reached a mission station by the name of Nia Nia run by a tubby Italian pere. He welcomed me into the mission without reservation and let me set up camp in its centre, which was in the process of being built. That night I was disturbed by the sound of what I took to be people creeping around my tent; I built up a cold sweat of fear and decided to take action. With a screwdriver in one hand and my camera flash in the other I dashed out of the tent half naked to find a thick mist but nobody around at all. Lighting a sorely needed cigarette I decided that the noise that had woken me probably was due to condensed water from the mist dripping off the surrounding trees onto the various piles of building materials and creaking of the tree branches.

In the morning as I was preparing my morning porridge in my ex-army aluminium billycan I was greeted by Hans, a traveller who had been staying at the Hotel Olympia. He and his girlfriend, Haniker, had left town the day before me and he was after some petrol from the mission for his cooker. Later that morning, about 3km out of Nia Nia, I rounded a bend on the jungle track and encountered Hans and Haniker walking along the track

On a typical jungle track

View down the track

with packs on their backs. I stopped and we chatted again for a while; they were emphatic that this was the only way to experience the jungle and see its wildlife properly. Of course, they were probably correct, as the noise of any vehicle is long heard before it arrives, and jungle creatures are notoriously shy.

By lunchtime after a slow and rough ride through very thick jungle full of exotic birds, monkeys and baboons, I arrived at a place with the unforgettable name of "Station de Capture D'Epula", which roughly translates as "Place of the Capture of Okapi". At the far end of the village by a babbling river was an old ex-colonial house, complete with stoep, which was now being used as a World Wildlife Research Station. At the back of the house was a mini zoo and a couple of specimens of Okapi ,this beautiful and shy jungle creature were kept in an enclosure for research purposes. They look like an elegant cross between a zebra and a large buck, such as a kudu. In another cage they had a rather forlorn-looking chimpanzee, not a happy sight for me, I would much rather see them in the wild or not at all. This place dated back to 1928 when an American anthropologist founded it as a capture station for okapi to be sent to American and European zoos. In 1997, the okapi wildlife reserve was listed as a World Heritage Site in danger. In 2012, a Mai-Mai rebel

Up the track

Monkeys ahead

Dried out potholes

attack left all of the centre's fourteen okapis dead. It is estimated, however, that the reserve might have 5000 okapis surviving within it.

Back in the village after a restaurant hut meal of rice and meat of undefined origin I decided that the patron's generous offer of a girl and a room for just $2 was not for me so I left for the next village 50km further up the track. Mambassa was a sort of jungle district centre with two little Asian-run trading posts and a nice mission station run by two friendly and welcoming Italian priests who invited me in to share their evening meal of potatoes and excellent cheese from Lake Kivu. Strange or maybe not, to see pictures of Italian football players and teams adorning the walls of their living room. One of the priests was also an artist who travelled around Africa from mission to mission painting murals and frescoes on church walls. They told me the only good thing about President Mobutu in their eyes was that he was a Catholic. Otherwise they told me he was possibly the richest most corrupt leader of any nation in Africa with millions of dollars of aid money and international loans ending up in his Swiss bank account. In the village at the priest's suggestion one of the Asian shops was able to supply me with petrol but at a high price of £4 per litre, so I purchased just five litres, enough with what I had left I thought to get me to Beni.

After Mambassa the road became about the worst I had encountered in all of Africa; it was in a wretched state not helped by the previous night's rainfall. Huge potholes stretched in a series over the next five miles; these monsters were of the legendary truck-swallowing kind, up to 12ft deep and varying from 10ft to over 20ft long, lined with thick, gooey mud at the sides and pooled at the bottom with brown water. For me the only way through them was to plunge in and at all costs keep the wheels turning in the mud grooves of the previous truck where a few stones and pebbles lay for traction for forward momentum. Wandering from this groove would have ensured a swift bogging down in no time. Finally, we encountered the pothole to end potholes, the one with my name on it, so to speak. It was over 20ft long and as I rode into it the front wheel and forks disappeared into its water. The engine was under water and making a strange whirring sound but amazingly still providing power enough for her to keep moving in first gear. The water was so deep it was lapping my saddle and at the far end of the crater we climbed slowly up onto a sort of mud hump and as the engine broke air once more a huge cloud of steam burst away from it and one cylinder ceased to operate. I switched off the ignition and pushed her through the next hole and onto a patch of dry ground. I was convinced that there would be serious damage to the engine such as a cracked cylinder head, or water being sucked into the carburettors, but not a bit of it. Just a quick change of sparking plugs while being watched by a group of villagers who had gathered in no time and were asking for cigarettes, and then we were off once again.

The late afternoon found me close to a place called Mount Hoyo. I followed a sign and turned off the trail up a bumpy rough jeep track which climbed steeply up through several pygmy villages. At the top there was a surprisingly smart hotel with incredible views over the miles of steaming jungle and I discovered that I was their first visitor for ten days. I made camp in the hotel garden as I had no need for a room and agreed a small fee with the hotel manager to have use of the ablutions.

The following morning as I wove down the steep track to the waiting jungle below, passing back through the pygmy villages I noticed that the pygmy men had the most extraordinary tattooed faces and the women were all bare-breasted. Some, the shyer ones, took to their heels wailing at the very sight of me; others, braver, stood by the edge of the road and even waved, some chased after me. It was mainly the surprise of my presence that caused the panic for the little people of the forest.

At this point I feel that it will be of interest for the following extracts sourced from Wikipedia (https://en.wikipedia.org/wiki/Pygmy_peoples) to be brought to your attention:

It is estimated that there are between 250,000 and 600,000 pygmies living in the Congo rainforest.

African pygmy populations are genetically diverse and extremely divergent from all other human populations, suggesting they have an ancient indigenous lineage.

The pygmy population was a target of the Interahamwe during the 1994 Rwandan Genocide. Of the 30,000 pygmies in Rwanda, an estimated 10,000 were killed and another 10,000 were displaced. They have been described as "forgotten victims" of the genocide.

From the end of 2002 through January 2003, around 60,000 pygmy civilians and 10,000 combatants were killed in an extermination campaign known as "Effacer le Tableau" during the Second Congo War.

The extermination was carried out by soldiers from the Movement for the Liberation of Congo (MLC), who became known to locals as *les effaceurs* ("the erasers"), and troops from the Rally for Congolese Democracy.

The primary objective of *Effacer le tableau* was the territorial conquest of the North Kivu province of the DRC and ethnic cleansing of pygmies from the Congo's eastern region whose population numbered 90,000 by 2004. The Bambuti were targeted specifically as the rebels considered them "subhuman", and it was believed by the rebels that the flesh of the Bambuti held "magical powers". There were also reports of cannibalism being widespread.

In March 2016 the International Criminal Court found Jean-Pierre Bemba guilty of human rights violations in the Central African Republic. Bemba was the vice president of the DRC, and leader of the MLC during the year-long extermination campaign, but was fully acquitted by the ICC's appeal court in June 2018.

It appears that these lovely shy people have had a really terrible time since my journey through their domain.

Later that day after some great jungle scenery I climbed out of the jungle for good and pulled into Beni, the first civilised place I had encountered since Kisangani 400 miles behind me. My immediate need was for petrol and there was a garage on the roughly tarred high street, but the news was no petrol was expected until maybe the following week. The lad in attendance however advised me to go to a large logging company further down the road just on the fringe of the town. There I encountered a fat director with flashing gold teeth who refused to sell me petrol unless I could pay for it in either pounds or dollars. In exchange for one of my few remaining notes he gave me a permit, which I took down to the pumps to exchange for fuel. The chit was however for more fuel than the bike could hold so I asked for a refund credit note with which I doubled back to the director's office. Just after he had issued me with a credit note for the accounts office a police Land Rover screeched to a halt in the compound yard outside his office. Clearly in a panic he called for his door to be shut and grabbing his radio started to talk at speed in French in an agitated manner to Kisangani. I had no idea what was going on but did not like the signals I was reading so decided to forgo the cashing in of my credit note and leave immediately, not wanting to get caught up in a developing situation. I thought also that I had heard somebody say in French that I was the cause of the situation!

Perhaps someone had seen him take my foreign currency and he was being done for it?

I walked out of the office's back door keeping my eyes cast down as I passed the police in the yard and strode out purposely to my bike unchallenged. I was greatly relieved when we passed out of the compound's gates and rode as fast as I could for the next two hours to get far away in case I was going to be arrested.

The low mountains close to Butembo were becoming increasingly beautiful and I reached the town just after dusk and found a cheap dive just off the centre of town which had a small mud-walled room to offer. Suzy was also allowed to stay in the dining room, which saved me having to unload the bike. In the morning a very cheerful maid was surprised to see a Mzungu cooking his own porridge and pointed with a smile at her own bouncing coffee-coloured toddler enquired, "This is yours"? As I prepared to leave, the bike and I were surrounded by about thirty children all bursting with questions and I exchanged addresses for the hundredth time with the Patron, who was a nice man. All in all, a very pleasant place.

The road south continued, very rough and bumpy, being mainly constructed from gravel and rock, but the views were incredible, reminding me of the foothills of the Alps, and the air wonderfully cool in the early morning; at one point we climbed up as high as 2341 metres. I was surprised to pass green fields with barbed wire fencing and European-style farmhouses, perhaps of Belgian origin; also I rode by several coffee and timber plantations.

At around 11am I crossed the equator at the village of Musienene, but there was no sign to say exactly where the line lay. That afternoon the roughness of the road took its toll on my front tyre, which punctured whilst at slow speed. I could see that this tyre was beginning to break up into cracks on the inside surface, which would then pinch the inner tube, so resorted to my old trick of placing a rubber patch over the cracked areas as well as repairing the inner tube.

After 6pm I arrived at the very edge of the "Grand Escarpment de Kabasha" where a pole barrier lay across the road. From there on the road wound tortuously 4000ft down the steep escarpment to the Virunga National Park below. The barrier shut at 6pm every night, so the gateman explained to me, but for the price of a cigarette the pole was raised for me and off down the mountain I went with my destination being a game lodge a few kilometres inside the park. The descent was very spectacular but the road so steep it was heart-stopping. The savanna plain below was vast and stretched as far as I could see in the early evening light with the horizon obscured by the approaching night.

After 18km of sharp bends the track straightened out, levelled and stretched out in front of me across the plain. Just at the bottom I saw my first herd of elephant, a small group of six magnificent beasts standing not 50m from the road as if to welcome me. It was a strange and beautiful encounter, too exciting by far to have me worried. I remembered then though that I could not linger as night falls quickly on the equator and the park was also notorious for both lions and poachers, so after a few minutes of savouring this incredible moment, I swiftly rode on past them. Later I spotted a second herd, again very close to the road, though I could not stop to admire them.

On the road many large bucks took flight almost at the last minute as I unexpectedly approached; fortunately the huge black-horned buffaloes I also saw were some distance away. The lodge appeared to be smart and expensive, had no running water, but did offer a swimming pool. The receptionist unexpectedly offered me a girl for the night, but I declined, saying that I was too tired!

Leaving at 8am I had just passed the hotel's entrance guardhouse when I noticed deflation of my front tyre; by noon I had the tyre repaired and prayed that it would hold good for my trip through the rest of the game park. Over the remaining thirty-odd miles I saw more elephant, many different types of buck, warthogs, baboons, fat black hippos, but no lions; perhaps in the heat of the day they were asleep. In truth I must say I was relieved about that!

Virunga National Park Road

Shrouded in clouds, the 4507m volcano of Karisimbi loomed up and then also to the right of me, that of Nyiragongo at 3470m. This had to be some of Africa's wildest and most spectacular scenery, rightly now on the World Heritage list of endangered places, and for the many years since my trip, pretty much off-limits to tourists due to security issues with various rebel groups fighting over Lord knows what.

Out of the park, as we approached the volcanos, the track surface turned into a real backside bruiser, particularly where lava streams of grey, blue and tinged with pink had solidified over the road over large distances. Eventually as we neared Goma's airport a tarred surface took over, smooth as velvet by contrast. I celebrated rolling along, carefree with no hands on the handlebars, singing a song and feeling highly elated.

At Rwindi Lodge I had met a young Belgian couple who had very kindly invited me to stay at their house at Goma, which was also the residency of the French Consul although they would not be getting back home for a couple of days. The guards there were good and allowed me to pitch camp in the villa's garden and showed me where to shower and get water. Breakfast was a fabulous bowl of fresh strawberries brought to me by the houseboy; I felt comfortable once more after an arduous journey of six days from Kisangani.

Goma lay on the edge of Lake Kivu, the first of the freshwater Rift Valley lakes I was to pass. It was surrounded by the spectacular backdrop of high and active volcanos. In a bar in town I ran into travellers I had met before on the trail down; together we made a plan to try and climb Nyiragongo the next day. That evening, my hosts Paula and Daniel arrived back from safari in their Land Rover and were most hospitable. Daniel had worked previously for three years in Niger before coming to Zaire and currently was working for the United Nations Food and Agricultural Organisation engaged on research on Kivu's volcanic soil. He told me that the land here was incredibly fertile and the climate so perfect that anything could be grown here in multiple crops all the year around. He predicted that one day in the future Kivu province would be able to feed all of Zaire and more. He also informed me that Zaire at that time due to corruption and mismanagement was unable to feed itself and was importing meat and fresh products from South Africa. Sadly, forty years on that remains the case for so many of the nations of Africa; the continent should and easily could be a breadbasket for the world.

I arose before the sun and made my way to the agreed rendezvous with my fellow mountaineers for the climb. After coffee we managed to hire a battered old Peugeot to take us to the foot of the mountain where there was a footpath leading up and a group of guides eager to provide their services. We engaged one and started our ascent walking across lava flows that divided the thick woodland of the lower slopes. After an hour I had to pause for nature's call and from then on at regular thirty-minute intervals all the way up to the summit. The effort was intense for me as I was doubled up in pain with cramps but continued to persevere feeling weaker all the time in the thin air. My climb rate diminished to that of an old man, taking fifteen steps and then pausing for a minute to catch my breath. It was merciful that in my whole trip through Africa this was the only real inconvenient loose guts moment that I experienced. After four and a half hours' climb, we summited so to speak by emerging onto the actual rim of the volcano and were greeted by an incredible vista. Directly below our boots was a 500-metre sheer drop down a cliff to the centre of the crater. It appeared as a giant open cast quarry, over half a mile across to the other side; clouds of steam wafted up and the air was heavy with the sulphurous stench of rotten eggs. The descent took about five hours and by then I was feeling very unwell and was averaging a squat session every ten minutes. Just before dusk we reached the track to town and managed to flag down an ancient Ford pickup with already twenty people plus goats and sheep on board to get back to town. In order to save fuel, the driver would turn off his engine on every downslope and freewheel down helped by a couple of boys to maintain momentum and maximise the distance that he could then travel on the flat until the next incline.

On the crater rim – Nyiragongo

Back in Goma the next few days passed very pleasantly in the great company of my Belgian hosts. There was tennis, dinner parties and swimming trips to the lake shore with beautiful clear blue water, so pure one could drink it as one swam. These expats made sure they had a really good lifestyle here. Although somewhat detached from the reality of the outside world, it was a pleasant place to be and I was very well looked after.

Once more after a very relaxing week it was time to leave. A couple of kilometres along the lake shore heading east I reached the Zairian border post. There were no problems with the currency checking and forms, etc. as the post was manned by an avid motorcycling fan who had a huge poster of a 750cc Honda dominating the mud wall of his office. No-man's land was about 1km and then at the Rwandan border the problems began!

Chapter 13

RWANDA

"NO, IT IS IMPOSSIBLE TO CROSS, YOU HAVE NO VISA, YOU MUST GO TO UGANDA." I was however experienced to know that in Africa anything is possible and that no statement however authoritarian should be taken as gospel. I spent all day waiting patiently trying to keep all and sundry at the post entertained and even sharing the border guards' beers with them as they extracted wads of money in bribes from the passing local traffic. It was 4pm, eight hours after arrival, as all hope was fading and even a rare attempt at bribery had failed, that the border officer called me back inside into his office, pulled out the necessary forms and visa papers and sent me on my way. It had been an exercise all along of him demonstrating his personal power in his personal fiefdom.

Later in Kigali I met a Brazilian traveller who had had exactly the same experience with this official and had been kept, heels kicking so to speak, for two days before being admitted to Rwanda.

Rwanda is one of the smallest, most mountainous and most densely populated countries in Africa.

A lovely stretch of new tar highway led up and down the valleys full of fertile banana plantations to Ruhengri. When the road was at altitude the air had a champagne-like quality to it, being fresh and pleasantly cool. Then the road changed to a dirt track and was amazingly dusty, in places to a depth of nearly a foot, which made riding pretty hazardous; probably this was volcanic dust as the neighbouring volcanos were active. Whenever a vehicle passed, I was forced to halt and wait five minutes for the dust cloud to settle.

Kigali is a hillside capital, modern in appearance and busy with traffic. I had hardly encountered city traffic since Nigeria two and a half months before. The local people seemed to be quite accustomed to seeing Europeans on the streets. Just off the centre of town was a cheap mission-run hostel which I had heard about on the traveller's grapevine, which was occupied by travellers and also refugees from the recent war with Burundi. The mission was run by nuns and they allowed me to lock my gear in a safe room adjoining their office as theft was likely otherwise.

Already I was missing the casualness and warm unpredictability of Zaire and I realised sadly that now I had left the excitement and uncertainty of the centre of the dark continent behind me. I was now emerging into a developing part of Africa deeply influenced by the Western outside world.

Looking for the British Consulate I was assured by a young man that he knew the way; as the bike was unloaded, I put him on the back and followed his directions. We ended up on the far side of town where he pointed to a new industrial building with a newish Volvo saloon car parked outside and said that this was the consul's car. Sceptically I said farewell to this crook who had conned me into a free ride across town. Inside the building of course nobody could help me.

Back in the hostel dormitory that night a slightly drunk old man, one of the Burundi refugees, spent the entire evening staring relentlessly at me endlessly smoking eye-watering cigarettes. He spoke only Swahili and could not understand why I could not converse with him. There was no point in telling him not to be so rude and to stop staring at me, for he was ignorant and too drunk to understand. I was left with no option but to reflect upon the plight of so many animals caged in zoos throughout the world for the pleasure of staring people.

I had been planning to visit Uganda since the mad despot Idi Amin was no longer in power having been deposed two years before, and I had heard that it was a very fertile and interesting country to travel. However recent travellers' tales that I had heard about robbery and theft by officials made me conclude that it would be very dangerous for me to ride across solo. This also meant that my plans for Kenya and seeing Nairobi would have to be abandoned too.

Kigali was tiring me rapidly, a city with no heart or soul and its inhabitants were not the nice gentle folk I had ridden so many miles to see. After a halt of four days I eased away from Kigali and rolled gently down the tarred hill towards the Tanzanian border, a cold and hilly ride but with great views. At the border there was no one around and the barrier was down and padlocked. After I had spent a couple of hours admiring a tumbling waterfall at a bridge in no-man's land the officials eventually returned from a late lunch and allowed me to pass after extorting a £4 toll fee for crossing the bridge over the river.

Chapter 14

TANZANIA

T HE TANZANIAN OFFICIALS WERE VERY FRIENDLY AND SPOKE GOOD ENGLISH; IT was another marked reminder that I was now leaving French-speaking Africa for good after what had seemed to be a very long time. The hills were steep, dry and brown in what I discovered was the classic East African feature of the countryside in the dry season. The road was a dirt track, at times well-groomed and at others, roughly corrugated and rutted. After a while the track became a new road which had no direction signs and did not appear on my trusty and very reliable Michelin map no 155 of Central and Southern Africa. However my compass bearing indicated that it was heading in the correct direction for Lake Victoria and the shore city of Mwanza, 200 miles away to the east.

At dusk I had not passed or seen a soul since leaving the border some hundred miles back. I passed a large troop of some thirty baboons, which led me to believe that there probably would be lions about. This must have been one of the least populated areas of central Africa; I covered mile after mile of country with simply no one around. The hills became gentler and finally, as I was limp with weariness, I came to a roadworks encampment with a couple of friendly watchmen left behind to guard the equipment.

They were both armed with large bows and arrows which they proudly said was for defence against lions. I had been right to worry after all! "Simba check," they said in Swahili; they had no English. They asked me to pitch my tent right in the middle of the culvert under construction so that I should be even safer from attack with only two approaches for them to guard from attacking lions. That evening we sat enraptured by the brilliance of the stars and gorging on huge chunks of spit-roasted meat; they enjoyed with particular relish the cigarettes I was carrying.

In the early morning the workforce arrived just as I emerged bleary eyed and yawning from my little green tent. They were surprised to see me and when I explained that I had no Tanzanian money, their foreman, a Tamil from Sri Lanka, very helpfully exchanged some shillings for a few US dollars. He then dashed off in his pickup and returned after half an hour with some fresh bread and bananas for me for my breakfast, after which he insisted on refuelling Suzy with a free gift of his company's petrol.

We covered many more miles up and down many hills covered with dry brown scrub on the very rough surface of the unfinished road and then, not to my surprise, the rear wheel punctured. A jolly old boy of about eighty years old squatted by the roadside to watch me make the repair with great interest. I found that the new puncture exactly lined up with a new large crack growing in the inside wall of the tyre, which was now pinching the inner tube. After the two-hour job, the repair only held for two miles but by then I was close to the centre of a town called Geita.

As I sat dejectedly smoking a cigarette a pastor on a little Honda stopped and suggested that I stay at the nearby mission hut; the bike was willingly pushed there by the crowd of usual volunteers. The guest house was a complete surprise; the room they had allocated me had a mosquito net and clean linen on the bed. However, the shower was a bucket which had to be filled up with water from an old oil drum in the yard.

In the evening a chap approached me out of the darkness and asked if I wanted to buy some gold from the local mine. Knowing nothing about gold, nor wishing to fall in with any dubious characters, I decided not to pursue the matter.

At dawn I repaired the puncture and attended to patching the crack as thoroughly as I could; there were many more miles yet to cover of rough roads before I would be able to find a new replacement tyre. I spent half an hour waiting patiently in a queue of government Land Rovers at Geita's only petrol station but then gave up when the news broke that the fuel pump was no longer working, and fuel was having to be hand-cranked. I decided that I had just enough to get to Mwanza 150km away. One of the government drivers told me I was a "lucky dog" to have got so far without being attacked by robbers or wild animals.

The terrain was once more hilly, covered with dry brush scrub and small thorn bush trees, and the road very corrugated and bumpy. Closer to Lake Victoria the track turned to a sand base causing me to slow down considerably. At Busisi was a large ferry to enable the crossing of a large neck of the lake. I noticed a group of lepers sitting to the side of the road cheerfully sharing a joke as they waited with hands outstretched for any gifts from the ferry queue.

The boat was much less primitive that the previous ferries I had encountered and getting on board was no problem at all for they had a proper drive-on, drive-off ramp. The only issue was the vast number of people, lorries, buses and other vehicles grossly overloading the vessel. Later that year I read about this ferry capsizing with severe loss of life.

On the other side it was a slow crawl for five miles on a dirt track in the heavy ferry traffic to then join the tar highway leading to Mwanza. Mwanza was a pleasant trading port but in decline as current relations were not good with Kenya and a trading embargo was in place. Before that it had also been subjected to bombing raids from Idi Amin.

A friendly Sikh at Kigali had given me a contact name for a friend who was working at the city's bus company. Sikhs are the transport boys all the world over and the contact, when I found him, immediately said that I was welcome to stay at the repair depot a couple of miles from the town and ordered his son to escort me there. The repair depot had a small first-floor room which had a total air of dilapidation about it but as the depot itself was fairly secure and guarded I felt that it would be safe enough for Suzy and my baggage. The walls were shedding peeling paint, there were no curtains, some old and holed wire mosquito netting over the unglazed window openings, a soiled and stained bare mattress on a springless bed, and a bare concrete floor with old scattered newspaper pages. The water supply was intermittent but, in the evening, I was able to take a much-needed shower after the depot watchmen had washed; at least it was free.

In the town I found a tailor who was able to stitch up my disintegrating luggage bags; the advantage of soft luggage, it is easy to get repaired. As I was riding back to my lodgings, I chanced upon a Suzuki 250cc machine parked outside the city library, the first I had seen anywhere on this continent. I parked beside it and a chap rushed out of the building and told me I could not park there. I calmed him down and was told that the library had purchased three of these bikes new in 1977. This made me think that there would be a good chance of finding more spares in Dar es Salaam. For the past few thousand miles I had been running with a front disc brake on metal against metal contact only, the pad having worn out back in Cameroon.

Inside the library I met a VSO worker, a young Norwegian called Liara who very kindly invited me to join up for supper with some friends that evening who were also involved with VSO work in Mwanza. After meeting in the early evening for drinks at the New Mwanza Hotel, Liara drove me out in her VW Beetle to her English friend Mary's house right on the shore of Lake Victoria. Mary was an English teacher and was from Portishead; the meal was excellent and accompanied by some strong red wine. Also at the table was an English VSO worker called Dennis from Manchester who was also a biker and pleaded with me to delay my departure until the weekend so that he, Mary and another friend could accompany me on their motorcycles on the next leg of the journey to the town of Shinyanga, 150 miles to the south.

Smoke break on the Shinyanga Road

Dennis turned out to be a bit of a character and invited me to relocate from the bus depot to his huge colonial-style house, again on the lakeside shores, which he was looking after for a doctor away on holiday. The house was a short walk away from the Mwanza Club, a crumbling old colonial relic well past its better days, however, as well as its good cold beer it also had a wonderful swimming pool recently filled with fresh water.

Pete, Dennis's friend, had a small Honda trials bike and arrived just before midday, so the three bikes headed away from Mwanza in convoy for what turned out to be a magnificent run down to Shinyanga, crossing an endless, gorgeous, brown burnt open plain. We passed many hump-backed cattle grazing alongside the road attended by a few herd boys and towards evening were treated to another wonderful golden-orange sunset with eventually the whole sky turning to fire, probably due to all the dust in the atmosphere. It was great and memorable to have the company of fellow bikers on this stretch and to share the magnificence of outback Africa. As night fell, we roared into Shinyanga and found the house of a teacher friend of theirs without too much trouble.

First job of the day was to track down fuel for my next stage; the first petrol station had no fuel and the second would only serve fuel if a government petrol permit could be evidenced. I got the all-important "Kabali", as the lad from the garage guided me to the

On the road to Shinyanga – Mary, Dennis and Pete

The road goes on

government office where it could be obtained, and it was issued to me with no trouble, being a tourist.

The ride I planned for the day was 300km to the town of Singida. There were many corrugated sections on the dirt highway and after the first hundred miles my backside was aching; there were no punctures, thank God. I took a good half hour lunch break of bananas with bully beef under the shade of an acacia tree and admired the surrounding scenery of brush scrub and gentle rolling plains. There were very few inhabitants on this remote road and little traffic; I passed a few troops of baboons to keep me company. After eight and half hours I pulled into Sigida feeling exhausted after the near 200 miles of jolting highway.

In the town were a surprising number of brightly painted guest houses. I picked an excellent one which also had an internal courtyard in which to park the bike, so saving me the trouble of having to unpack the bike. A very welcome double Tanzanian whisky and ginger ale gave the energy to look for food; however, the news of fuel in the town was bad, with no supplies expected until Monday, two days hence. Dipping my tank back at the guest house I thought it was touch and go for the next likely fuel opportunity 200km away but decided to give it a shot anyway the next day. My fear of having to push the machine was not helped by a local in the bar warning me of a wild and dangerous tribe living along the road to Babati, my destination. Perhaps he was bullshitting or maybe I wanted to believe that he was!

After a great brew of my Africafe, possibly the world's best instant coffee of the era and made in Tanzania, I climbed aboard once more and set out into the cold morning air encountering a strong headwind, which would put further strain on my fuel consumption. The road climbed over the next fifty miles rising up to nearly 3000m by the flanks of Mount Hanang and I nearly froze to death. The Maasai herders I saw were wrapped, huddled up as mummies, in brown blankets and carrying hugely long lethal-looking spears as they guarded their herds of grazing cattle. They were friendly enough and waved to me as I passed, which was a relief to me after the discussion of the previous night.

Many flat-topped acacia trees grew on these high plains;, it appeared to be similar to the Serengeti, only a hundred miles to the north from here, but I passed no game at all. The peak of Mt Hanang was concealed by clouds and I knew not if it had snow.

After many more miles than I thought possible to squeeze out of my tank (it had been over 320 road miles since I had last refuelled and there remained a little fuel to spare), I arrived at the dusty crossroads town of Babati and I promptly celebrated by indulging in a hut restaurant meal of rice and meat as tough as old boot leather. The place was fly-blown but churned out unlimited cups of sweet brown tea. Once again, I found an excellent small guest house and my "Piki-Piki", Swahili for motorcycle, was allowed inside as well.

Amazingly, they had charcoal-heated hot water for me to shower away my aches and pains.

On the Monday, petrol was obtainable on demand at the town's garage; however, after refuelling I noticed that my rear tyre was going flat. I guessed that it was either a slow puncture or else grit in the valve. Extracting one sparking plug I screwed in my invaluable air pump into the left-hand cylinder head and fired the motor up on the right-hand cylinder. The tyre would take about three minutes to come up to its correct inflation pressure, and the whole operation by now I had down to about five minutes. Re-inflated I set off at speed for the last fifty miles of sandy track before the velvet carpet of luxurious tar leading to Arusha started. The jolting from the rear became much more severe so I was forced once more to stop and change the inner tube. By the time, two hours later, I had completed the roadside operation I was surrounded by a crowd of onlookers who had popped up seemingly from nowhere. Just before the job was done, a police Land Rover, overtaking a crawling water tanker on a blind bend, nearly ran me down. At the last moment they spotted me and swerved back in behind the tanker, leaving me shaking and my heart pounding, another close call. The previous occasion of near disaster had been back in Cameroon when a wildly careering earth scraper, being driven much too fast by a probably drunk driver, came around the bend, saw me and plunged off the track to dig another road!

My relief and achievement on reaching this long-awaited strip of tar was immense; from here onwards if I wanted to I could, according to my Michelin map 155, ride all the way down to Cape Town, 5000 kilometres away. This though turned out not to be so, as many of the roads indicated in both Tanzania and Malawi as being sealed were ploughed up and now returned to dirt, presumably because of lack of upkeep since the end of colonial days.

Just after hitting this strip of tar I had a chance sighting of my first ostrich grazing on the pasture of the plain. According to my map this road ran between Manyara National Park on my left and Tarangire National Park on my right. The beauty of the landscape and my sense of achievement was such that I burst out in song all the way to Arusha. Suddenly a hilarious thought came to me that my motorcycle was really a very comfortable armchair on wheels that had transported me across Africa, just as a gripping film on TV takes the viewer out of his seat and into the picture.

Diary note, 26th August 1981 – 12,191 miles from Bath to Arusha!

At Arusha I had been given the address of a friend of Dennis and Mary's back in Mwanza. Mike Dixon was a very hospitable and easy-going "Taffy" who liberally dispensed such goodies as Tanzanian whisky and cigarettes, easily consumed by my hungry body. I stayed with Mike Dixon at St Constantine's school for the following day enjoying his company, humour and a whisky-fuelled evening touring his favourite bars of Arusha.

Leaving Suzy and my gear in his safe keeping, I embarked on an early morning bus ride up to Ngorongoro Crater.

After sitting in the local bus for the next two hours with every seat taken, the bus driver finally decided that it was hot enough to consider departure. We then spent the next half hour driving around the town and ended up at a garage on the opposite side of the town to Ngorongoro and refuelled. After the total of three hours delay, we then commenced the journey for the crater.

It was a very long hot ride, a bumpy, dusty, fly-infested experience. Suzy would have been 1000 times more preferable, however it was an interesting experience. At every other mango tree or hut the bus would stop to load more people, children, chickens, goats, etc. on board.

They were mainly Maasai and most had the wonderful aroma of cow dung, which they used with gay abandon as part of their make-up. Truly the world's foremost cattle tribe, amazing to look at with long hair finely plaited and ear lobes, necks and arms loaded with many layers of silver rings, coloured beads and ornaments. I was fascinated and at every

Ngorogoro Crater showing lake

jolt of the bus the ornaments dangling from the earlobes in front of me were so heavy that they bounced up and down many times as if suspended on brown rubber bands. Some of these even reached down as far as the shoulders. Without exception the hairstyles were striking, highly individual and undoubtedly had tribal significance.

They were a friendly people, but very proud, keeping their eyes largely averted from me, one of only three Europeans on board. They have managed to keep their way of life pretty unchanged but adapting it as it suits them to the modern world surrounding them. Many wore sandals made from discarded motor tyres and obviously the bus was a convenient form of transport.

The ride to the crater took all day and as the sun was setting, we climbed up the lip of its ring.

An old Maasai sitting behind me leaned forward and tapped me on my shoulder and said "Ngorogoro", eyes alight with pride and excitement, as if he were saying that this was his home and that I was welcome there, pointing for me to look at an incredible view right into the heart of the crater in the darkening light. The fleeting glimpse of the vista was so magnificent that it made me exclaim out aloud. The hazy blue of the depth of the crater all but hid its floor, giving the impression that inside the crater there was sky. Vaguely I could see the far rim of the other side, then it was gone as the road dipped down once more.

Around the next bend we saw a large herd of the biggest, most evil-looking black buffalo I had ever seen grazing by the side of the road. Seeing the whites of their eyes of Africa's most dangerous of beasts was heart-pounding, even from the safety of the bus window. At a distance they seem as innocent as a herd of Jersey cows; the herd was stretched over a good mile and must have been over 300 strong. In addition, three elephants were forced off the road by our bus; now I could understand why motorcycles were banned from this park, I would not have stood a chance. Finally, a lion was spotted by some of the other passengers just before the night descended and in darkness we pulled to a halt after a long ten hours to cover just the hundred miles.

It was impossible to know where we were in relation to the tourist lodges as most tourist visitors here are conveyed by luxury bus or private car. All that was visible in the night was a cluster of paraffin hurricane lamps on either side of the road. I strolled with a German couple who had also been on the bus towards the nearest lamps. An old lady welcomed us and showed us a really filthy room in her hut which we could have for the night at a ridiculous price. The Germans decided to stay at one of the luxury lodges for the night as there seemed to be some sort of monopoly operating amongst the rest of the villagers as to the price for the night at their huts. I decided to take a lift with the game warden who was taking the German couple to "Crater Lodge". The ride through the African night on the open back of his pickup was sheer magic; we passed buffalo, lion, and buck of all sizes including a very small duiker who stood in the road totally blinded, as a wild rabbit caught in the headlights of our pickup. After dropping the Germans off at the mini metropolis of Crater Lodge the warden kindly transported me to a much older lodge where I was able to obtain a comfortable room for a fair price after negotiating for it for thirty minutes!

Early next day, as no transport was going, I walked up the driveway from my hotel to the track leading back the five kilometres to Crater Lodge where I knew that I would be able to get on a tour down to the crater floor. I noticed a couple of black buffalo grazing as cows in the distance so decided rather than continue to walk that it would be prudent to hitchhike from this point. After a few minutes a passing delivery truck stopped and gave me the lift up to the Crater Lodge resort. There I met up with my Germans who had already engaged a Land Rover and driver for the day and were keen for me to join them and contribute towards the cost. In the open topped Land Rover we bounced down the steep rough access track winding towards the floor of the long extinct volcano through the early morning mist. All at once we emerged from the cloud

No telephoto lens here

Mum and cub

The early morning kill

to see the crater floor looming up below us. It appeared as a large green plain, dotted here and there with herds of grazing game, and in the centre a shimmering blue lake. This was tinged at its sides with pink, which we later discovered were flocks of tens of thousands of flamingos.

Just after the track reached the crater floor, we passed a herd of wildebeest, a strange-looking animal with powerful front quarters and shaggy manes. Then we passed jackals, hyena, herds of grazing zebra and buck, and after that a pride of lions who had made a zebra kill in the dawn and were still gorging. The old male lay on his back as a huge kitten, one paw flopped on his swollen belly. It must be hard work keeping his nine lionesses in order plus the five cubs comprising his pride. We passed not three feet from them, which again sent my heart pounding; few of life's experiences are as exciting as close encounters with wild game. They would have had no difficulty in leaping into the open Land Rover as we were standing up, poking our heads out, taking our photographs. It was fascinating watching the cubs at play, stalking each other through the tall grass and then being scolded and put in order by their mothers.

Picnic lunch was taken in a shady forest surrounded by thieving monkeys and distant grazing elephants; a pair of courting ostriches were also spotted.

In the afternoon we were extremely lucky to see three black rhinos, with very long evil-looking horns; at the time, there were only thirty-five of these magnificent creatures left in the reserve. (Happy days, in 2020 there are thirty-five-plus black rhinos in the crater reserve.)

As we climbed back out of the crater, we lurched around a bend to come face to face with a huge lone bull elephant standing right in the middle of the road. We screeched to a halt and waited for him to move on. After a while a warden's Land Rover came up behind us and edging past us headed slowly towards the magnificent beast to encourage it to move off. With no warning the bull flapped its ears out, giving a loud trumpet of rage, then tucking its trunk into its mouth proceeded to charge the warden's jeep. Shaking its giant head from side to side the animal descended towards us as the warden's jeep flew past us at speed in reverse. Our panicking driver fumbled with the ignition keys and just in the nick of time our engine fired, and we too were fleeing backwards at speed around the bend we had come from. Safely away, we stopped, expecting the bull to come around the bend after us at any moment, but he did not follow through and when after ten minutes we gingerly went around the bend again, he was nowhere to be seen.

The travel back to Arusha in a Swedish couple's Peugeot was much more comfortable than the bus and just took three hours. They were both working as Voluntary Service

Charging bull

Please engage gear!

Overseas volunteers, as were so many other Europeans I met out in Tanzania, and they invited me to look them up in Dar es Salaam.

After a couple more days relaxing back in Arusha and several more whiskies with Mike, I left heading east on a good stretch of road towards Dar es Salaam via Moshi. There was thick low cloud and worse, light rain to spoil any chance of a view of Mt Kilimanjaro, which was a great disappointment to me. I even rode right up to where the trekking expeditions to the summit departed from, and still the clouds obscured the mountain completely. Seeing on the plain below a shaft of sunlight breaking through, I rushed back down in the hope of being able to look back up and see her snowy crown. All I could do to console myself was take a photo of the clouds around "Kili". The evening brought me to rest at a lovely old colonial hill station called Lushoto where I located a comfortable guest house just out of the town for the night.

It was a mountainous and treacherous gravel track of 19km descending back down from Lushoto to the main Dar es Salaam highway. In several places this supposedly tar-sealed highway had been ploughed up and returned back to gravel status and with the volume of traffic using the road it was not at all a pleasant trip down until we met the junction with the Great North Road connecting Zambia to "Dar". There the road was a beautiful smooth

Kilimanjaro – somewhere in the cloud

new highway without even the odd pothole to keep me on my toes. I discovered to my amazement that Suzy was still capable of doing 60mph, even fully loaded as she was. After an hour I glimpsed a far, tantalising glimpse of blue water, the Indian Ocean. It was a treat to see after covering so many miles across the interior; ten weeks ago I had last been at an ocean, the Atlantic coast at Kribi, on the opposite side of this immense continent.

Outside Dar lay a huge and ugly sprawling African shanty township through which I threaded my way towards the centre of town, and due to the good directions, I was able without much difficulty to find my Swedish friend's apartment building. Before turning in I decided that to deter Dar's notorious thieves from taking Suzy by removing her front wheel and taking it up to the flat. A simple but effective five-minute job. This was the most effective solution against bike theft that I could think of.

Dar es Salaam was a hot, sticky cosmopolitan city with no shortage of mosquitos. It might not have been as exciting as Nairobi and Kenya, which I had very much wanted to visit, but had been precluded by the border closure due to the collapse of the East Africa Community talks, but I was not disappointed by the experience of being in a large city once more after so many months in the wilds.

Down in the vast city market on my second day in Dar I found replacement front and rear tyres for Suzy; the new rear one was 50mm wider than specified but had a good knobbly patterned tread which just missed the bike's swing arm by 2mm. This extra-wide tyre was to perform exceptionally well in road-holding on the few dirt roads I had yet to ride on my journey south. These tyres were to take me to Cape Town and beyond in the years to follow. They were only removed from the bike in its restoration of 2018 and I have them now in my garage as a keepsake.

That evening my hosts, Johann and Eva, invited me to join them and some friends for an open-air movie in the grounds of the American consulate nearby. It was a strange experience to see a New York gangster film in the setting of another world; that of course is the magic of cinema, its transportation of the mind from the here and now.

My hosts the following day told me of a certain market in the town where it was possible to sell absolutely anything. I took them up on this and wagered that I would not be able to sell my completely worn-out old tyre casings, cracked, multi-patched and threadbare as they were.

The very first stall I approached offered me 60 shillings for the pair, much to my surprise, nearly half of the price that I had paid for them new in Cameroon some months before. I took my hosts to the best hotel in town and I treated them to beer and hamburgers with this windfall.

An Indian barber performed that afternoon an excellent pruning of my wild mop of hair; he was one of that breed of barbers met the world over who have the habit of talking non-stop to his clientele. It was very interesting to hear his tales and gossip of Dar. One poor innocent bystander was killed just two days before whilst standing outside his shop by a ricocheting bullet from a policeman firing at a black-market cinema tout who had refused his stop-and-search request. Johann, my Swedish host, was also repeatedly telling me stories of the theft and robbery in the city against the European community. Apparently, many expats here carry guns for their protection, although getting the police permit to bear arms was difficult. I continued to immobilise Suzy at night by bringing in both her front wheel and battery.

After four days in Dar I decided that now was the time for a holiday and leaving my hosts with a few non-essential items to look after for me, headed north up the coastal road to a camping resort known as Silver Sands, a well-known overlanders' holiday spot and a cheap good place to stay.

The sea was temptingly blue and the soft sand really was silver; security should have also been good with so many European holidaymakers around, but that proved not to be the case, for stories of losses abounded. One camper told me he had all his clothes stolen from his tent whilst he was sleeping in it. That afternoon two trans-African overland expedition lorries pulled in, each with a dozen or more overlanders on board; the camp was now overflowing with travellers.

It was strange to meet so many Westerners in one go after so many months in the infrequent company of just a few. Some were fresh out of Europe, others up from South Africa; I was deluged with the usual enquires as to how I had travelled and what was I doing in Tanzania on a motorcycle? I had learnt by now to face these repeated questions and to reply as enthusiastically as possible, although it could be quiet wearying. I now realised that in the future these barrages of questions from puzzled onlookers were going to become more and more frequent as I travelled closer to my destination of South Africa. Some were even rude enough to photograph me without asking.

At Silver Sands the days slid by in a leisurely way, cold ocean dips in the ocean, a stone's throw in front of my pitch, black coffee, bananas and bread for breakfast followed by sunbathing and further dips. One day I teamed up with a German film producer to buy the largest lobster I had ever seen in my life. We borrowed the largest cooking pot that the hotel possessed and it took over two hours to boil it to pink over my small petrol stove; the beast was more than enough to satisfy the two of us.

At night we would take turns in two-hour shifts from dusk to dawn to keep guard over our tents; this was despite there being a permanent submachine-gun-armed guard

Road warning sign – close to Mikumi National Park

Taken from the saddle

watching over the site. He was always asleep anyway and was probably in league with the local bad boys. The system worked well with a minimum of three people on duty at one time; sometimes intruders were heard trying to creep up to the darkened campsite and when challenged would melt away into the night. It was enough to keep us on our toes, but nobody lost anything in the five nights of my stay there.

After five days I felt refreshed enough to consider going back to Dar, where I stayed with my hosts Johann and Eva one last time before heading south-west on the Great North Road towards Zambia.

The tarmac seemed to stretch out in front of me forever, but the scenery was never dull, plains and ranges of hills spread all around to the far horizon. The traffic was light and the only thing to really watch out for was the odd pothole. It was wonderful to be motoring at consistent uninterrupted speed of 50–55mph mile after mile and my mind was able to drift and ponder on other matters far away from the trauma of focusing on potholed and corrugated dirt roads.

A high point of the ride was when the highway passed through the middle of the Mikumi National Park and to the side of the road were elephant grazing in the tall grasses, a most glorious sight which forced me to stop and take some photos and enjoy a cigarette whilst savouring this seemingly timeless vista from the saddle of my motorbike.

By evening I had reached a small and ugly hilltop town called Iringa where I found a rather dirty guest house. The depression of the place deepened when I discovered that there was no beer to be had anywhere, an African first. Over rice and tough meat in a locals restaurant I met a nomad from Ethiopia who had left his country after all his camels had died in the drought that sealed the fate of Haile Selassie, the "Lion of Africa". A desire for education and work had led him south to socialist Tanzania where strangely for a Muslim he was also decrying the lack of beer and cigarettes.

As I was at breakfast at the shabby guest house, I was apprehended by a plain-clothed policeman who asked to see my identity papers. I suspected that the owner of the guest house, who had generally acted in an unwelcoming manner the evening before, had put him on the alert. After politely answering a few questions and waving my passport under his nose, he became less hostile and suspicious of me and his tone of talk changed from, "I do not want to expel you from Iringa but…" to even "Why not stay in Iringa for the week?" After I had had a second more successful attempt at breakfast I loaded up as fast as I could and speedily left before any more trouble arose.

The road from Iringa to Zambia led endlessly up hill and down dale through some very dry and arid country and after some 200 miles we reached the border post and passed out of Tanzania with no issues.

I had to pass through a short stretch of Zambian territory to get to my target of Malawi; the Zambians at their post were all splendidly attired in spotless white uniforms, setting off the rich colour of their skins. Reams of forms had to be completed and again all money that I had not concealed had to be declared and counted meticulously. It was a lot of work to do to enable me to cross through just sixty miles of their country. Overall, they were professional, friendly and courteous, addressing me with "sir" on every question. However, I nearly cracked up when they could not resist playing with my full-faced helmet, one of them even removing his cap and trying it on, which also disconcerted me as I had a stash of dollar bills stuffed away inside its felt lining!

It was after 4pm when I was back on a dusty orange-yellow sandy back road that led east to the Malawi border, riding fast to try and reach the post before sundown and closure. The route wound slowly in gentle sweeping bends up and down shallow, slightly undulating hill country and the sand track started to become red, burnished by the sinking sun. Isolated villages dotted the route, in one of them a large black hen had a very unsuccessful skirmish with Suzy's headlamp. The silly creature, instead of staying still in a position of safety on the far side of the track where it had been pecking at the dirt, chose to make a determined rush to head straight into my path, her clipped wings enabling her only to lift off in flight as high as my headlight. Amongst a cloud of feathers, I looked into my wing mirror to see a dark lump lying still in the road behind me. "Why did the chicken cross the road?" but perhaps this was not the moment for a jokey riposte.

Soon after sunset I arrived at the padlocked pole that marked the end of Zambia. After enquiring at a few huts, I located the Immigration Officer who willingly unlocked the pole for me, declining to look at any of the papers I had spent an hour of the afternoon so carefully filling in. After covering ten miles of no-man's land in complete darkness, I arrived at the Malawian border pole.

Chapter 15
MALAWI

AFTER A FEW MINUTES ALONE AT THE BORDER POLE A VILLAGER CAME UP AND asked me to wait whilst he found the border post official. After about half an hour a customs man arrived, but there was a price to be paid for the late disturbance of his peaceful evening; he asked to inspect all of my luggage after dealing laboriously with my other documents. As he wished to see all of my possessions, I asked him if I could sleep the night on the porch of the post, which he reluctantly agreed to. Then began the arduous task of opening up all of my luggage for his inspection. When he saw my books his eyes lit up and he rushed back into his office returning with a highly treasured list of books which were banned in Malawi; it was dated 1976. Placing all of the books that he had me extract from my backpack in a pile, he then proceeded to check every single one against his list to see if they appeared. The last one in the pile was *Africa on the Cheap* by Geoff Crowther, and gleefully he said that he would have to confiscate it. After all this nonsense I was getting a bit annoyed, for I was tired after the 350-mile ride, hungry and determined not to be outdone by bungling officialdom. I remonstrated with him, asking how he could confiscate this book as it had only been published in 1980 and therefore could not be on his list. He said that they always confiscated these types of guidebooks and that I must now wait at the border all night so that his boss could have a read of the Malawi section in the book in the morning.

I was lucky that he was not able to read English well for the book was highly critical of Dr Hastings Banda's Malawi and likened his Pioneer corps to the Hitler youth movement. It was in my view irresponsible of Crowther to write this in a book likely to be carried by overlanders into that country. One can spend time in jail or suffer worse on a lesser charge in Africa and he surely should have realised that. No way was I going to be around for his boss to read this in the book, so way before dawn I packed Suzy up and did my first and only illegal border crossing by just riding around the padlocked pole and quietly on through the sleeping village with the night sky turning grey in the pre-dawn light.

It was a wonderful morning ride up and down small mountains without a village or anyone by the road for more than seventy miles. After first light the sky turned blood orange, then suddenly the sun rose catching the mountaintops and highlighting the gentle wisps of mist floating below in the valleys. The rugged terrain was a dusty dry-season brown, typical of that time of year in East Africa. There were many acacia and other bush scrub trees, some in flower, and the odd baobab. The first settlement the corrugated dirt track brought me to was Karonga, lazing on the northern shores of Lake Malawi, a magic stretch of enchanting blue water, to me the finest lake in Africa.

As I rode up to the town's crossroads a neatly dress policeman stepped out from behind a bush and flagged me down. Naturally I thought the worst; had the customs post people radioed news that a mad white man on a motorcycle had gatecrashed the border? But no, he asked the usual "Where are you going and coming from?" then surprised me by asking why I did not have a number plate on my front mudguard. I replied that the motorcycle was registered in England and that we did not allow number plates on the front of motorcycles because of the danger to riders and pedestrians in the event of an accident. This seemed to satisfy him but before letting me continue he asked to hear my horn, which was still operative, loud and clear.

After a further 50km run along the lake shore it occurred to me that I should be looking for a bank to get some Malawi kwacha and also fuel, as I was getting low. The last fuel had been purchased back at Mybeya, Tanzania, some 200 miles behind. I cut my speed back to 30mph to help consumption. After passing a pretty lakeside fishing village called Livingstonia, there was an incredible 3000ft climb up steep hairpin bends to a pass on the Nyika Plateau. The view of the crystal-clear blue lake far below from here was breathtaking, with the mountains of Mozambique over fifty miles away clearly visible. My dwindling fuel supply was fast eaten up by that climb and a further deviation of 40km to the small town of Rumphi where I was hoping to find a bank and fuel. Once there the locals informed me that the mobile bank only visited once a week and that the next visit was due in four days. There was no fuel available here either and without local currency it would have been difficult to get in any event. There was nothing to be done other than turn around and carry on towards Mzuzu, a large regional town some fifty miles away. After some forty miles I had to switch to my reserve petrol supply tap and ride with a continuous swirling motion for the last fuel drops in my thirty-three-litre tank to trickle down the fuel pipe to my twin carburettors. Two miles outside the town I passed Mzuzu airfield and it was here, after some 350 miles since Mbeya in Zambia, that Suzy ran out of petrol for the first time in the entire trip. The date was September 13th – what a coincidence.

Having slowly covered the first mile pushing on my own on a fortunately flat section of road, a couple of eager lads ran up and volunteered their services, which I very gratefully accepted. They pushed me all the way up a hill into the town and on to the government rest house, which was very comfortable with, joy of joys, a bed with blankets and clean cotton sheets. I had not met such luxury since leaving England five months before. It was also a great pleasure for me to find on the dining room table that evening a wide selection of condiments including Heinz tomato ketchup and HP Sauce. Funny how one comes to relish these trivial things when one has done without for so long.

After the bank opened and I had obtained a good pile of kwacha notes I pushed Suzy down the hill to the town's petrol station. I was surprised to find a long queue of vehicles there wating for the pumps to open, so I pushed the machine to the front of the queue to find out what the delay was all about.

At first the manager said that there was no petrol available and that ten days had passed since they last were restocked. I explained that I was a stranded tourist and that it was urgent for me to reach Zomba that day. He told me to push the bike behind his sales office and there he very kindly filled Suzy up from his emergency reserve supply, to my intense relief. This once more reaffirmed to me that in Africa, usually, where there is a will, there is a way. Also never believe one hundred per cent what one is told. All the way south the petrol shortages continued; Mozambique was once more flexing her muscles over some petty dispute or other and had cut back on the monthly fuel train to Malawi up from the port of Beira. The previous day, as it turned out, I had been incredibly lucky to have run out of fuel only two miles away from the only source of petrol probably in the whole of Northern Malawi.

The day's ride was most enjoyable, Malawi being possibly the prettiest of African countries I visited, plenty of lush jungle-clad mountains and gorgeous lake views, all well complimented by the friendliness of the Malawians. I predict some time in future years it will experience a complete tourist bonanza but for now it remains a rather wonderful undiscovered place of paradise.

The route south soon descended from the highlands down to rejoin the lakeside at Nkhata Bay and on for a hundred miles of more sandy corrugated dust as it wound its way along the shoreline through tea gardens and banana plantations interspersed with many fishing villages. The inhabitants were incredibly friendly and waved and smiled as I sailed past them. They are very poor people even in comparison to the other African nations surrounding them, but their poverty seemed to give them a virtue not found in other deprived peoples I have encountered of the world. It is because they are people gifted with an inborn pride and self-respect and live off the proceeds of their own hard work.

Malawi at that time – without any mineral wealth to speak of, its economy centred around agriculture and fishing from the lake – was one of the very few countries in Africa to be self-supporting; it did not rely on huge UN food and agriculture aid programmes as many of its neighbours did.

After the lovely ride of 360km, taking it slowly to conserve fuel, I arrived at Salima to be met with the most welcome news that the town had just received its first supply of petrol in two weeks, so I headed straight to the garage to drink my fill. I located a cheap bed for the night in a hotel next to the bus station and found a great chilled bottle of "Elephant" beer. A drunken paratrooper ruined the peaceful evening by trying to drag me out to a nightclub; I was far too tired after the nonstop 1000-mile ride from Dar es Salaam to appreciate the idea.

The thin strip of tar I found myself on next morning led me back to the lakeshore and onwards towards the delightfully named lake port of Monkey Bay. This was the last town before my destination, a beautiful camping site at Cape Maclear. Here I found an excellent market and shops full of produce and some imported luxuries from South Africa. Whilst stocking up at the market I dropped a banana, and in a flash, a ragged bent old man picked it up. I thought that he was going to eat it or ask for money, but no, with a smile revealing half rotten teeth he gave it back to me saying, "For you, sir," and walked away. So much for my arrogant assumptions born of a "superior" civilisation; I was indeed humbled.

Once more well stocked, I rode back to the spur track which leads to the peninsula of Cape Maclear, 20km of sandy track away. Soon the brilliant blue of the sparkling lake, dotted with small forested islands, filled the horizon as the track wound down a short hill to an old colonial hotel nestling in a secluded cove on the lakeshore. This hotel had long been out of commission, but the site was a famous spot for campers and the bar was still operating serving snacks and ice-cold beer to the tourists who frequently came here. The place was a delight and so I decided to stay for a week "on holiday".

Around the corner from my tent pitch was a series of small rockpools known as Otter Point; there, a myriad of blue, green, orange and gold tropical fish danced, shimmering in the crystal-clear water. I was able to take a picture of them by pointing my camera a couple of feet above the water's surface, such was the clarity of the water. Swimming in water that pure and purportedly Bilharzia-free meant that one could drink it as one swam. Indeed, all water for drinking was just decanted straight from the lake by those camping around it.

On holiday at Cape Maclear

The week passed only too quickly, typically I would start with cleaning my teeth in the lake just after sunup, then an early morning swim followed by breakfast of fresh coffee from Tanzania, porridge with bananas and on one occasion fresh mulberries provided by a fellow camper. Usually a fisherman would paddle his dugout to the shore adjacent to my tent and invite me to buy some of his early morning catch; "Chambo" was my favourite, being very flavoursome, with good flesh and few bones. I would then gut, impale on a stick and tenderly grill the Chambo over my open fire for lunch. Sadly now, in 2020, Chambo has been over-fished to such an extent that it has now been listed as an endangered species and is "red carded" as being in danger of becoming extinct.

After the afternoon feast I would take a siesta under a shady palm tree, then perhaps swim around the Otter Point or go for a long walk down the lakeshore to the nearby fisherman's village. In the evening most of the campers would gather around in small groups to chat and admire the stars, to swim for hours in the still warm lake, floating and gazing upwards at the wonderous constellations above, later drying off beside the warmth of a good campfire. How simple and easy was this way of life, I could not think of a more heavenly holiday for me at that time of my life.

Strange rock markings off the track to Cape Maclear;
my hair is swept back as I rode the track that day without my helmet

After idling away the best part of eight days I decided reluctantly that it was time to load up and get on the road again and see some more of Malawi. The road led on southwards to Mangochi towards Zomba, the old capital of what was then Nyasaland, and current residency of the Life President, Dr Banda.

The heat was building as I arrived at Zomba. In the centre of town was a large square surrounded by shady trees, which was operating as the town's market, full of fresh product stalls, flower sellers, cloth merchants, tailors, and even metalworkers. I remember watching them, with fascination, beat some scrap metal forming it into a bucket. My stocks were again low and pretty much everything I wanted was available here and in the adjacent grocery store. This was in stark contrast to what I found to be available in Tanzania or Zambia.

The campsite I wanted to stay at for the night was 5000ft above the town on a mountain that dominates the town and is known as Zomba Plateau. It's a huge plateau of some 130 sq km and has several peaks; the highest rises to over 2000m. Curving its way up through avenues of jacaranda trees, luscious jungle and forests of pine tree plantations, the narrow

Tomato seller, Zomba Market

tar single-vehicle width road climbs up to the plateau and then circles the plateau. It operates as a one-way system changing from uphill direction to downhill traffic every two hours as there are very few places for vehicles to pass each other. On reaching the top, a large clearing in the shady pines revealed a welcome campsite.

Soon after pitching my tent I wanted to explore this new, almost European-like terrain of trout-filled streams, pine groves, mountain peaks and hidden valleys. I walked out onto the mysterious plateau, so different to anywhere else I had encountered to date in Africa, and hiked to the very top of the closest mountain peak, appropriately called Sky View. There I watched eagles swooping among the cliffs below over a gigantic yawning chasm falling seemingly sheerly to the brown plains below.

That night was cold due to the altitude; the surrounding pines blotted out all sound except for the occasional hooting of owls. There was only one other tent up here, belonging to an English family, Jack and Alex and their two delightful daughters, on vacation from Blantyre, the commercial capital of Malawi.

In the morning I freewheeled down the hill for twenty minutes to save fuel in blissful silence. In the old marketplace I found a cobbler to repair my luggage bags once more.

Campsite, Zomba Plateau

Whilst he was doing the repairs, I refuelled and then rode around the lower suburban roads on the lower flanks of the plateau, a wonderful place to reside with many bungalows with fabulous gardens carved out of the jungle on the hillside. Small winding, climbing roads lined with beautiful blue flowering jacaranda trees and green bamboo shooting up over 20ft tall, interspersed with patches of jungle and the flame of the forest trees with their near-scarlet plumes of blossom really made the route appear to be completely exotic. Dominating the approach to this residential area was the Old Gymkhana Club, rising as a proud relic of past imperial days sitting on the edge of an immaculately maintained green cricket pitch.

Inside the club all was hushed and orderly, a cool breeze blew under the huge mahogany awnings which swung open to allow members at the bar to enjoy the cricket. As I sipped a very refreshing rock shandy I could not help but reflect how artificial this scene was in the heart of such a wild continent. Also how incredible it was that empire had succeeded for so many years to bring schools, transport infrastructure and employment to such a remote area. I felt a definite pride in those days of empire for our part in this extraordinary

Gymkana Club, Zomba

and beneficial development of the interior of this amazing continent, despite its obvious failings.

My musing was interrupted somewhat rudely by the appearance of some of my fellow countrymen dressed up to the nines for their lunch with ties, jackets, creased trousers and polished shoes, braying to each other in cut-glass public-school English and entirely ignoring my presence. Not even one of them attempted to say hallo, only a couple of the Malawian members had had the courtesy to say that; maybe the holes in my jeans and lack of tie made me out of place. I found it unfriendly to say the least; for an Englishman not to acknowledge the presence of a fellow compatriot so far away from home was damn rude.

Having relaxed for a couple more days on the plateau I decided that I wanted to explore more of Malawi's incredible mountains, in particular Mt Mulanje, famous for its scenery and mystique. I rode ninety miles south to Blantyre and there was able to leave Suzy in the care of Jack and Alex who also kindly loaned me a detailed hikers' map of Mt Mulanje and a collapsible fishing rod. I decided that it would be best to hitchhike the fifty odd miles to the mountain's base; my first lift on the road out of Blantyre was from a Taiwanese diplomat, whom I mistakenly thought to be a communist after he told me his country was the People's Democratic Republic of China (not mentioning Taiwan). He was most amused when I explained this to him and as we laughed his driver swerved violently, just missing the car we were overtaking, which had decided to make a right turn without indicating.

After a few kilometres they dropped me off and I then flagged down a taxi bus which took me to the town of Thyola. After failing to get a lift on from there after two hours of trying, every passing vehicle being too overcrowded to stop, I decided to try and catch a bus from the town's bus station.

After sitting for thirty minutes in the twenty-year-old vehicle, literally exploding with people and chickens, the engine roared into life and we started another long and tedious journey. The bus groaned to a halt at every village to deposit and take on board crowds of women and children loaded with bulging bags and animals. I had the hilarious idea that one passing mama as she squeezed by might catch the hook of my projecting fishing rod and reel the line out all the way up the bus, what confusion that would have caused!

Tired and blinking in the bright light of midday I crawled out of the vehicle to find myself in Mulanje village and found a lovely chilled bottle of Coca-Cola in the village store, it's the best of restoratives when you are tired and overcooked in a hot climate. Finishing a second bottle I shouldered my pack and began the 10km hike to the mountain's base. Pulling my battered old Vietnam bush hat low on my brow I trudged doggedly under the midday sun, sweat pouring as a cascade from me, proud to be living up to the legend of "Mad dogs and Englishmen go out in the midday sun."

The view across the neatly cropped verdant green flat-topped tea bushes made the intense heat worth bearing. There was no traffic on the narrow winding dirt track; as I rounded a bend I met a party of young boys and girls, dancing, clapping and blowing whistles as they approached. They swept me up with them, pack and all, making me dance with them before releasing me to continue on my way; Africa provides a surprise a day.

Towards evening I arrived at the forestry office where I was able to find a comfortable bed for the night and where also I obtained a licence to fish in the mountain's trout streams. As my leg had turned a little lame on the day's walk, I was also able to book a porter to carry my pack for me the next day on my planned trek up to the mountain's plateau.

At 7.30am next morning my porter arrived, keen and eager to start the expedition. We brewed some tea and then started the climb, up and up towards the sky. After three hours we emerged at the edge of the plateau by a crystal-clear pool which I eyed with anticipation, thinking of the borrowed rod in my pack. From the edge of Chambi Plateau it was another half hour walk through a plantation of tall mature pine trees before we came to the mountain hut, a delightful lodge constructed of local cedar. Having paid off my porter I spent the rest of the afternoon soaking up the beauty and solitude of the mountain, which I now had exclusively to myself. From my hut I could see across a spread of green pines to the peak of Chambe, soaring way above into the blue sky. The hut was spartan, sparingly furnished but comfortable. A stone hearth fireplace was prepared, and a stack of dry cedar wood was provided adjacent to it. That evening as the night drew in, a single match was all that was required to start a roaring blaze without the need for any paper. I kept the fireside company that night reading by its glow a compendium of short Kipling tales another hiker had left behind.

A small man with a badly pockmarked face arrived at the hut just before dawn and introduced himself as the fishing officer for the plateau. To my annoyance he insisted in accompanying me to the stream below; after several attempts at being civil and amenable to the fellow, I had no option but to be sharp with him. Fishing is a most serious pastime and his garrulous behaviour was spoiling my concentration; soon he took the hint and left me in peace to the stream and its fish. The magic of the flowing water soon cast its spell over me, bubbling merrily through the quiet forest of giant pines. The water was cool and clear right to the pebbled bottom. The rainbow trout dancing below were plentiful but disappointingly small; after several changes of fly lures I landed my first catch at about

Dancers on the track to Mulanje

Dancers on the track to Mulanje

midday: a silver streak of about six inches long leaping and bounding on the end of my line. It took me another hour of casting before a second was hooked, then my luck turned and I failed to haul anything in despite one or two exciting bites. Within an hour of my return to the hut I was savouring quite delicious boiled trout washed down with tea laced with brandy.

I spent another peaceful night in solitude at Chambe hut and left the next day early for the five-hour trek across the plateau to Thuchila Hut. The view that morning surpasses description; Chambe peak was so clear that every rock of its massive basalt cap was highlighted with great clarity; apparently this peak offers the rock climber the longest rock climb in Africa. The path climbed steeply for a while then traversed across several valleys bristling with fabulously scented old moss-covered cedar trees. Around a bend without warning appeared no less than five mountain peaks rising in a parallel formation one behind another. The path I was on passed on the flanks of all of these peaks, one of which (Sapitwa) was ablaze with a bush fire, fortunately high above the path. At one point I saw in the mud of the path the spoor of a large cat, probably a leopard, which were known to be numerous on the mountain. I started to wonder what it would be like to encounter one on the path head on around a bend. This did not happen, but a couple of large grey-brown baboons gave me a hell of a fright jumping from tree to tree across my path. By mid-afternoon I arrived at Thuchila Hut, the oldest of the ten huts on the mountain, built in 1901 of Mulanje cedar and maintained by the Mountain Club of Malawi. It has a lovely setting with a long shady veranda and superb views across towards Zomba plateau some fifty miles away.

As the sun slipped away towards the horizon, the sky was burnished pink and gold, sinking finally as its last rays haloed the far Chambe peak close to where I had started my day. As night fell all the bush fires above me on the mountainside came to life in a line of flames running from peak to valley and on up to the adjacent peak, causing me some concern. The wind direction was away from me, but this did not prevent my sleep-drugged consciousness from pondering late into the night what I would do if the wind was to change and the fire came dangerously close to the hut. I was on my own up there on the mountain and probably there would have been no escape!

It was with relief that I awoke to discover that the fires had not altered their direction after all. I strolled on a gentle path offering incredible views over the plains below, which led to the edge of the plateau; from there the path seemed to just fall over the edge into a devil's staircase; missing one's footing here would have been disastrous so my pace of descent was cautious and slow. After ninety minutes I came to a jeep track and the going became much gentler. As I strolled there was a sharp rustling in the bush to my left; swivelling my eyes around I glanced a flash of green and yellow, a long thin green mamba had been disturbed by my footfall and literally just took off. Had it come my way I would have been "dead meat" with no chance of escape due to my pack and complaining knee.

Later that day I arrived back in Blantyre after another laborious journey by taxi bus, motor bus and an ageing 1950s Hillman Husky of exactly the same colour and interior as the first car I remember my mother driving when I was a five-year-old.

From Blantyre I left early on the third day on the road north back up through Zomba, bound for Zambia and the Victoria Falls some 800 miles distant by road; light rain and mist hampered my journey all the way back to Zomba. After that the mist lifted but the sky was overcast with thick heavy grey clouds; it was actually chilly riding through the mountains towards Lilongwe. This was the new modern capital of Malawi since 1975, replacing the previous capital of Zomba and constructed with the help of huge foreign loans with the idea that it would provide an impetus for the development of the central and northern parts of the country. Lilongwe proved to be a dull and drab city with a few featureless modern buildings of glass and concrete. My stay there was limited to filling up with fuel, changing money and collecting the mail. I found letters from my parents, brothers and sisters; sadly one bore news of the death of my maternal grandmother some five weeks before. This sad though not unexpected news occupied my thoughts for the rest of the day. Often she had looked after us as children and in turn my mother cared for her for many months prior to her admission to a nursing home in Bath. She had been a wonderful source of knowledge of an era now long past; one of her best bits of advice to me was never to get into debt. Her mind in the end had become completely childlike but mercifully she was unaware of her declining mental powers. She was eighty-nine years young when she finally gave up the struggle. I was very sad that I could not make the funeral though I had visited her in the nursing home in the week before leaving for my trip and sort of knew it would be unlikely that I would see her again.

Chapter 16

ZAMBIA, ZIMBABWE AND BOTSWANA

At the Zambian border the immigration officials noticed that my cholera inoculation certificate was out of date, however the conversation went around to that of changing money and the problem was conveniently forgotten. This was much to my relief as potentially a rusty needle could have been produced in this sort of situation and the end result might be serum hepatitis, or blood poisoning, or worse. They gave me a very fair rate of exchange of about twice the official rate, being extremely polite throughout the negotiations. Usually I would not consider a black-market deal with officials for fear of being "shopped", however I sensed no malice or connivance in the situation and as it was after banking hours, I needed the Zambian kwacha to enable me to continue on to Lusaka.

I was able to refuel at the border town of Chipata and rode on down the Great East Road mile after endless mile through very rugged, scrubby bush country. After dark I was still in the saddle and finally at about 8pm I pulled into a layby and pitched my tent, heavy with tiredness and aching from the long day's ride. Sixteen hours and 535 miles in one day, a record!

Just after dawn I started my daily maintenance schedule, cleaning and resetting spark plug gaps, oiling and tightening drive chain and topping up of two-stroke oil tank. A couple of drivers from a nearby lorry, which had broken down in the night, strolled over to me and were amazed to see my "house" in the layby. They were very surprised that I had chosen to spend the night there for they insisted that there were many lions in this area and they had not dared leave their lorry cab all night. Looking at my map I realised that there might have been some truth in what they were saying for the road ran alongside the vast Luanga Valley South Game Reserve and there were no fences around the reserves in this part of the world.

It was a long ride down to Lusaka; I pulled into the city about lunchtime. The surrounding rolling hills were burnt brown by the sun but the city was quite picturesque with blue flowering jacaranda trees and bright hibiscus hedges lining the route through the central business district. The centre of town was teeming with people, but the atmosphere was sultry and claustrophobic. After a quick stop at the main post office to collect my letters I rode straight out of town on the Kariba road. I passed dozens of huge ranches, the road being fenced continuously on either side, the first time I had seen this declaration of ownership of rural land in Africa.

After the turn-off for Kariba I carried on south-west on the long highway stretching another 500 kilometres to Livingstone. Suzy's power was noticeably diminishing and it was not due to the headwind either; on closer examination I found that one of her cylinder head gaskets had blown, probably caused by the exhaust being blocked up with carbon deposits and by the continual vibration perhaps loosening the cylinder head bolts over the many thousands of kilometres that I had travelled since this problem first manifested itself back in Algeria. I changed the aluminium gasket around and retightened the head by the roadside, but there was no noticeable difference so once more I pulled over and repeated the operation but this time using a new replacement gasket, which seemed to do the trick.

Once more I made camp a few kilometres outside Livingstone in what was probably lion-infested country, but I was too tired to give it a second thought.

Livingstone was a hot and dirty town. I checked at the post office for mail but after explaining for ten minutes to a nonplussed official what 'poste restante' was he proudly showed me their box containing just one letter. It must have been lying there for several years by the look of the dust covering it. The last of my kwacha were spent on food and the luxury of ice cream at the nearby somewhat run-down Intercontinental hotel; ominously, above the bar hung a poster of a hangman's noose and the slogan "For those who talk". Obviously a relic from the Rhodesian bush war which had been raging here just two years before. Beyond the hotel lay the Victoria Falls Eastern Cataract, a short distance through the Livingstone National Park. My first sight of the falls was impressive but by no means as spectacular as that I was to experience later on the Zimbabwean side. Unfortunately, at that time of year (October) the summer rains had yet to fall so the Zambezi was fairly low and this had been a year of drought. However, a huge plume of spray hung over the falls area doing full justice to the legend of "Mosi-oa-Tunya" ("the smoke that thunders") as the natives had described the falls to Dr Livingstone a century before in 1855. At the

The Victoria Falls from Zambian side

The Victoria Falls from Zambian side

top of the falls was a luxuriant tropical rainforest abounding with creepers and lush plants not normally found this far south in Africa. My visit was somewhat marred by an local rushing up to me and excitedly asking, "Have you seen the body, sir?" "What body?" I replied. "The body of the suicide victim," he responded. I retorted that I had actually come here to see the falls, not suicide victims. I found out later that some poor girl had thrown herself over the falls a week before; no one had been able to recover the body and later it was hoped that the flow of the water would be strong enough to wash it downstream.

At the border with Zimbabwe, the Zambian customs and immigration officials were very interested in my journey through Africa, so much so that after I had been processed they all trooped out of their post and lined up in their immaculate white uniforms and caps to wave me off over the bridge to Zimbabwe. It was a great moment.

At the Zimbabwean post a glaring black official and a dour white one proffered papers by the dozen for my signature and asked a score of probing and irrelevant questions; the difference between the two posts was like that between a warm fire and a wet blanket.

Bridge over the Zambezi

After checking my possession of an air ticket, despite my assurance that I was touring Africa by motorcycle, they allowed me entry. The town of Victoria Falls was my first taste of being back in a modern world, contrasting sharply with the dilapidation of its neighbour, Livingstone.

The shops were surprisingly well stocked compared to any that I had seen in the previous five months. I nearly wept at the sight of fresh sausages, cheese, milk and butter. In the centre of town, I found a very well-planned campsite with clean ablution blocks for both sexes.

A recent coat of paint was covering the scars of a recent blast of attack mortars on the walls of the otherwise elegant and sumptuous Victoria Falls Hotel and a Marimba band was performing as I arrived for lunch. The Marimba is a huge wooden xylophone which is struck with rubber mallets to produce a wonderful soothing tone. I discovered that it was not necessary to top up one's beer for at the appropriate moment a white-gloved hand would shoot forward and perform the task. A suitable reward I thought after riding 1000 miles in the past three days.

Campsite at Victoria Falls

That evening a shady character called Ralph, who claimed to be an ex-Rhodesian soldier, offered me a good rate of exchange for my British pounds; he had been changing money with all the foreign visitors to the campsite with the idea of smuggling the currency back out of the country. At that time the Rhodesians who were emigrating were only allowed to take £50 worth of currency, a car and a minimum of household furniture out with them, not much to restart a life with.

Later in the evening I met up with a German tourist who was planning to hire a car to visit the Chobe game reserve across the border in Botswana and invited me to join him. I readily agreed feeling that the trip would be a welcome change after riding the bike for so long. Also I met a group of young South Africans who were planning to drive north to Zambia and on up to Kenya and wanted my opinion as to the need for taking a gun with them. Absolutely not was my advice, and I suggested that they handed their weapons into the police station for safe keeping.

Early next morning I took Suzy over to the Victoria Falls police station and explained my plans. The station sergeant was more than happy to store the bike for me in their car pound and was really interested about my trip down through Africa. It was a hopeful sight for the future of an integrated Zimbabwe to observe on my way out of the station a group of native and white policemen squad-bashing together under the watchful eye of a native sergeant.

On my return, Fiti, my German friend, was already back at the campsite with a blue Renault 5, which he had hired for our planned expedition. Victoria Falls was no larger than a village and surrounded by bush country; once we had turned off the main road at the top of town, the bush was all around us. The narrow road was of tar laid during the bush war years to make mine-planting more difficult and to assist border patrols.

Halfway towards the border we spotted a couple of elephants standing under the shade of a tree beside the road. Fiti pulled up parallel to them and turned off the engine. I took a quick photo, leaning across Fiti, pointing the camera out of his open window, after which I told him it was not such a good idea to be no more that 6ft from a bull elephant in a small car with no engine running to enable a quick getaway. My previous encounter with an elephant at Ngorongoro Crater had made me somewhat wary of these magnificent beasts. As instructed, Fiti restarted the engine and pulled a respectable 30ft away after taking on board my concerns. He told me that he had never before seen an elephant, so I related my previous experience to him. On reflection, I think that the only reason why the elephant did not object to our presence was due to the strong midday sun and the cool comfort of where he was standing. Certainly, for me, a heart-in-the-mouth experience and not the last one of that safari.

Car stopped and engine off!

Engine now running!

The border crossing presented no obstacles and the road became a rough corrugated dirt track. Kasane was a collection of a few administrative buildings, clusters of African huts and a safari lodge with petrol pumps. A few hundred yards from the hotel we came to the entrance of Chobe National Park.

After paying a small entrance fee, the entrance pole was lifted and we bumped our way slowly along a sandy track, rounded a bend and without warning we were surrounded by elephants. They were on all sides in groups of twenty to thirty with a few solitary bulls at the fringes. Obviously they were accustomed to vehicles for when the road was occupied by our car they would silently melt into the surrounding bush to move around us. It was really amazing how quietly these giant animals could just disappear, as if they had the power to become invisible.

The sand track ran down to run alongside the banks of the Chobe river; here the scrub was less dense and a clear view could be had of a pool full of hippos with tick birds on their heads, flanks and sides. We also came close to a large herd of some thirty elephant including mothers and their offspring bathing in the river. Young bulls squealed with

Spot the lion!

delight as they playfully squirted water at each other and baby elephants hid between their mothers' legs.

Beyond the river was a magnificent view of the Caprivi plains, my first view of South African administered territory. As the track left the river, we rounded a bend at speed to avoid getting stuck in a patch of soft sand. Stationary in front of us blocking the track was the first vehicle we had seen since entering the park. As the track was too narrow for us to pass them, we halted about 30ft away from them; without even thinking I climbed out of the vehicle to ask them if they could make way for us to pass. As I got halfway between the two vehicles a hand shot out of the passenger window and waved at me to go back. Simultaneously my eyes looked up into an adjacent bush to meet those of an enormous lion squatting on its hind quarters in the middle of the bush and looking directly at me. My heart rose into my mouth as I very slowly turned on my heel and walked slowly but purposefully back to the Renault, not daring to look over my shoulder and willing myself not to break into a run. With shaking hands I was able, once safely back in the car, to lift my camera and take a photograph of the lion in the bush as we drew parallel to it, where I had stopped and turned. Once more I was grateful for it being midday for if it had been cooler perhaps the lion would have felt the notion to play!

There was a basic campsite about 15km from the park entrance; it was primitive with two small shower blocks with a Rhodesian boiler (a wood-fired oil drum boiler connected to water pipes) outside. Mounds of elephant dung in the clearing testified to the lack of fencing of any description.

A troop of baboons and vervet monkeys played in the surrounding trees forcing us to have a scrupulous regard as to the safety of our food supplies. That night from the dubious safety of our tents we heard in the distance lions roaring, the hideous cackling of hyenas and high-pitched cries of jackals. It was eerie to think that a lion could easily be slinking around the camp, perhaps experienced in pulling an easy meal out of a tent and then peeling him out of his sleeping bag, as one poor camper I later read about in the Okavango, Botswana had the misfortune to experience; he did not live to tell the tale.

Before breakfast we took a dawn game run in the Renault, but compared to the splendid game we had seen the previous day, the sightings were sparse. We concluded that most of the elephant, rhino and buffalo were now far from the river grazing on more luscious bush than that left close to the heavily populated banks of the Chobe river. We did see a few bush pigs, their comic little tails sticking straight up into the air as markers as they sped away through the low bushes on our approach. Also encountered was a beautiful pregnant giraffe who gracefully strolled through the scrub stopping at trees to graze as the notion took her. Looking up to the sky we saw a flight of vultures wheeling

Rhodesian boiler

and calling to each other above the riverbank further on. As we drove towards them we experienced the most horrible smell of decay and then to our horror and disgust saw the bodies of three elephants lying on the bank. Their tusks were all missing, so obviously they had been slaughtered by poachers. The stench was overpowering and literally dozens of vultures were fighting each other on top and inside the distended bellies of the dead beasts, their beaks bloody from scavenging and their cackling and screeching at each other was as morbid as death itself. It was a shock to witness the results of poaching these noble beasts at first hand and one I had not ever expected to encounter.

That evening the wind got up and moaned across the Caprivi plains to buffet my tent. The baboons in the trees above were uneasy, screaming and chattering all night long. The dawn was grey and dismal for Africa, so we left early for the return back to Victoria Falls, a distance of an hour and a half, recrossing the border without incident. That afternoon, after a couple of hours' rest in the elegance of the Victoria Falls Hotel, we both went down to the falls to take our leave, a reluctant farewell. Just beyond danger point, in the rainforest by the falls, I looked up and gasped involuntarily in amazement, for there on the very edge of the falls on the far side of the ravine a pair of gleaming tusks emerged, challenging the might of the foaming white water. "Elephant," I gasped to Fiti. It was not just an elephant but a king of a beast standing on a rock platform right at the edge of the cascade. We were spellbound; it was no use bemoaning our lack of cameras for there was far too much mist in the air for photography in any event. Slowly the bull tusker turned around and shuffled off, melting away into the dense bush scrub behind. We felt very honoured and humbled to have observed this amazing spectacle.

Diary note, 12th October 1981 – 15,616 miles from home.

The following day I left Victoria Falls riding south and east along the Bulawayo road, an almost featureless strip of tar 200 miles long through the bush scrub and acacia trees streaming endlessly past on both sides of the road without even any villages to break up the monotony. The only interrupting feature was the bombed-out ruin of the appropriately named Halfway House Hotel and a few apparently abandoned homesteads surrounded by high-security fencing. It was on this stretch of road some eight months later that an overland expedition truck was ambushed and ten tourists were kidnapped and six were cruelly murdered by their captors when their ransom demands were not met. The politics of this incident indirectly led the following year, in 1983, to the start of the Gukurahundi massacres, which were conducted by Zanu led by the North Korean-trained 5th Brigade against the Ndebele in Matabeleland and taking the lives of an estimated 30,000 people. It is a matter of record that the current President of Zimbabwe, Emmerson Mnangagwa, "The Crocodile", was the Minister of State Security from 1980 to 1989.

After 278 miles my engine coughed and I discovered that the bonza tank was completely empty; my fault for cruising mile after mile at close to 60mph on a lovely tar road. The first vehicle I had encountered in perhaps fifty miles drove past me only minutes later, turned around and came back to see if I was OK. It was a VW Beetle driven by an elderly American missionary. He kindly let me have a few litres of his fuel and then left me after this good deed. Bulawayo surprised me with its hugely wide avenues, which I discovered had been laid out by pioneers less than a hundred years before, and the reason for the width was to enable them to easily U-turn their ox team-drawn wagons. I was further surprised to pass a Woolworths store almost identical to that one might pass back home in Britain. In the heart of the city was a large park surrounded by blue-flowering sweetly scented jacaranda trees, called Centenary Park, with a magnificently equipped campsite in the middle.

The next morning I visited the Natural History Museum of Zimbabwe and admired an enormous stuffed elephant reaching a full 12ft to its shoulder, the second largest mounted elephant in the world. After collecting my freshly laundered clothes from the camp char ladies I rode 50km south-east into the Matopos Hills, a small range of granite hills with some bizarre rock formations. As most visitors to the Matopos do, I made my way to "World's View", the burial place of Cecil Rhodes, which was a tranquil and mellow place known locally as "Malindidzimu" ("The Hill of Spirits").

Rhodes had died in 1920 in Cape Town, 2500 miles to the south, and his body was transported from there to Bulawayo by train and then by ox wagon to this place, where during the Second Matabele War he had walked unarmed into the Ndebele stronghold and persuaded the occupying Impi to lay down their arms, so ending the war in 1897. I could not help but think how badly his body must have smelt by the time it arrived at World's View over two weeks later.

Further on in the hills I discovered a deserted campsite whereby some miracle there actually was hot running water for the shower block. The moon rose early and brightly illuminated the eerily shaped rocks as I cooked up my Boerewors (Afrikaans – farmers' sausage), the first of many I was to consume over the years to come. It was nice to be on my own again but in this location a bit spooky, and also I felt somehow vulnerable, though the night passed without incident. I got the feeling that this place had been a very popular tourist destination before the Rhodesian war, but now had been left on its own for some time past, probably due to security issues.

It was a short ride to the Botswana border at Plumtree where customs and immigration formalities delayed me for an hour. They insisted on providing me with insurance and on stamping my carnet de passage document in the wrong place, and when I protested that

A View of the World – The Matopos Hills – Rhodes' grave

they had got things wrong made it pretty clear that it was not my place to tell them what was necessary and what was not.

The road from the border point changed from tar back to dirt all the way down to Francistown and the heat bore down as a sweltering mist. After Francistown, a new tar highway, then the only tarred road in Botswana, led on down southwards to Gabarone, the capital. A short distance outside of the town I came across a local youth sitting dejectedly beside a brand-new motorcycle. I stopped and asked him if he needed help. He had no idea why his machine would not go. I soon worked out that there was no petrol in his tank. His grateful smile was beautiful to behold as his engine sprang back into life after I had transferred some fuel over from my Bonza tank. He said that he had just purchased the bike that morning and had been told that the tank was full. He had not much of an idea which lever and switch operated what on the machine and on reply to his enquiry as to where I was headed, he looked incredulous when I said Cape Town.

The litter by the roadside of this principal artery was truly appalling, discarded beer cans every few metres all the way from Francistown and plastic bags everywhere blown about by the wind. I found this a noticeable sign that this part of Africa was entering the modern era and this was its signature of modern consumerism. A countryside swamped and fenced in by the mad process of materialism, a force uncontrollable in its desire to ravage and lay waste to even the most unpopulated areas of our planet. Those beer cans would lie there for years until the sun and wind turned them into a rusty dust.

Deciding to enter the White Republic by its back door, so to speak, I had by then crossed enough borders to know that it was easier to cross at the more isolated posts and much more fun! I enjoyed the courtesy and interest of the officials at these out-of-the-way places. So I turned off the highway just after Palapye planning to cross into South Africa at Martin's Drift. The road turned out to be no more than a sandy bush track running out from the vast Kalahari. It was a tricky trail to ride and I was approaching the state of exhaustion by the time I had covered the 100km to the border which, by the time I got there, had been shut for an hour. Further on from the post was a small police station impeccably laid out in the desert sand. It was the only sign of civilisation to be seen so I obtained consent from a rather bemused and not very helpful attendant to camp in their backyard. That evening I calculated that I had covered 16,255 miles from Bath to the South African border.

At 7am the next day there was already a small queue of locals waiting patiently for the Botswana border post to open. The customs and immigration officials were as pleasant, friendly and polite as I had predicted and within a few minutes allowed me to cross over the old iron bridge spanning the Limpopo river.

Chapter 17

SOUTH AFRICA

A	T THE IMMACULATE SOUTH AFRICA POST, GLEAMING WITH A FRESH COAT OF paint and, at the top of the flagpole, a neat orange and blue flag of the republic fluttering, I barged in through the wrong door to be greeted with a silent, startled and harsh glare of two well-proportioned Afrikaner female immigration officers, neatly attired in immaculate khaki uniforms. They made no demands at all to see any paperwork or flight tickets or foreign currency but merely stamped me in with a temporary visitor permit for three months' stay, simplicity itself. Perhaps being white was a help.

The tar started on the far side of the barrier pole and was virginal and over twice as broad as necessary. As my fuel was getting low and it was still over a hundred miles to Potgietersrus, I decided to flag down the first vehicle I encountered and try and scrounge a couple of litres of petrol. A huge "bakkie" (a pickup truck) soon came up behind me and I waved for them to stop; a couple of Afrikaner farmers inside were more than willing to top me up with some petrol and smiled broadly as I thanked them for such a generous welcome to the republic.

Potgietersrus struck me unexpectedly with the newness of its buildings and the sheer quantity of its shops and goods on display within; for goodness' sake, even the bank had an escalator to take you up to its portal. The other disconcerting thing was the speed of the traffic, though that was nothing compared to the rush-hour traffic I was to encounter later that afternoon as I pulled into Johannesburg, a vast city of glossy buildings not yet a hundred years old. The experience of packed modern traffic after six months in wide open spaces and isolation was quite traumatic, especially as earlier that morning I had still been in the wastes of the Kalahari, a stark and strange contrast, from wilderness to crazed urbanity in less than twelve hours.

A strange feeling arose, the warm glow of achievement filling me with elation, as I caught the first glimpse of Johannesburg from the national road from Pretoria. I wondered what the millions of people in that city would have thought had they known of my venture. A strange idea perhaps, but a real one to me at the time.

Gingerly weaving through the dense traffic, I found my way to Hillbrow; occasionally motorists, probably British expats, would toot their horns and wave or give a thumbs-up to me as they noticed my UK number plates and GB sticker, which gave me a tremendous feeling of accomplishment. To escape the traffic, I pulled into Zoo Lake, a public park next to the city's zoo, and at the lakeside restaurant phoned some friends who I had met the month before in Malawi and had invited me to stay should I make it to Jo'burg. They were out but one of the people in the house, which was a commune, gave me directions on how to reach the cottage at Crown Mines. I was there in half an hour; it gave me a nice warm feeling to know someone in a city of that size and to be welcomed.

Crown Mine Cottages

A few minutes after my arrival at 826 Crown Cottages, Ewan, my friend from Malawi, came home and we exchanged travel stories over tea. They were somewhat incredulous to see me and honestly admitted that they had thought that if the lions did not get me the "Ters" would. That evening it dawned on me that after so many months on the road the journey was ending and that I had started to "arrive".

The next week passed in a blur of readjusting to civilisation; the commune members without exception were incredibly kind, generous and hospitable to me, most were post-grad students and working professionals, all with strong Christian beliefs. I very much enjoyed the week I spent with them. They also socialised with another similar commune at no 820 Crown Cottages headed by a newly qualified doctor of medicine by the name of Julian who was on a sabbatical year after some traumatic experiences in attending to the victims of Soweto violence (he described being on shift at A&E as comparable to being in a war zone) and who greeted me, pipe lit (tobacco!), wearing a fabulous kaftan as if it were 1969. He turned out to be a most interesting and intelligent man, passionate about his hobby of discovering early bushman cave paintings in the Transvaal.

There were many wonderful evenings spent in earnest drinking, eating and endless revolutionary debate as to the future of South Africa and how things might pan out. They were very open with their views and opinions and often invited other students of mixed race and others to join them.

Even now I remember one young couple, white man, black girl, walking away arm in arm from the cottage after a great evening, and thinking to myself how brave they were to display such open affection in the middle of a defined white residential area.

We went to the movies one evening to see the blockbuster *Chariots of Fire* ("May you have wings on your feet") and, at the bar of the Market Theatre (South Africa's first multiracial cultural centre), the notable and also very controversial play for that time *Woza Albert!* After the performance we had a very interesting chat to the actors, who were also the co-writers, Percy Mtwa and Barney Simon, who I thought were incredibly brave to write and perform such a masterpiece whilst detainees were still flying out of the tenth-floor windows of nearby John Vorster Square (security police HQ).

Just ten miles down the road from Crown Mines Village was Soweto where I read to my horror in the *Monday Star* that "only" ten people had been murdered that weekend. The article went on to say that the average weekend murder rate was sixteen victims with the worst weekend of the year producing a total of thirty-six dead. Life, it would appear, was very cheap in Soweto.

The house was a delightful terraced cottage, red brick built about seventy years before, one of a small group of approximately twenty such cottages set out in two rows with an avenue of plane trees. The terraces were constructed to accommodate the skilled imported Cornish and Welsh miners who came out to start up the reef mines. The ground floor living room on whose floor I slept was embellished with exquisite pressed tin ceiling mouldings, and a fine tiled fireplace and timber sliding sash casements with glazing bars.

I called an old friend of mine, Sandy from Howick in Natal; he was overjoyed to hear me and simply amazed that I had made it. I had before departure sent him a letter from London giving him an outline of my plans; he had replied saying that I was mad to consider attempting the trip on my road machine and that I should consider getting a BMW off-road scrambler. When he received a postcard from me from Morocco, he knew I was on my way and he had made contact with the Suzuki Motor Company of South Africa, who had told him that if I made it, could I get in touch with them. This I was reluctant to do in view of the brush-off the company had given me in the UK when I had tried to explain to them my plans. After persuasion from Sandy, however, I relented and made a call to them, who suggested arranging for an interview with the editor of a magazine by the name of

No BMW for me!

Bike SA, and also offered me parts and servicing for the bike for the value of 200 Rand to assist with my onward trip to Cape Town.

On reflection I thought that this was pretty small beer. I got the feeling had I pulled into town on one of their latest models rather than a battered six-year-old GT 250 M, I would have got them to pay all the expenses of the trip! To put it bluntly, I was a bit of an embarrassment to them. South Africa at the time had two separate markets for motorcycles; the first was big, flashy, powerful and exclusively white. The second was for commercial delivery purposes and decidedly black, little machines of less than 200cc with carry boxes carrying freight and hurtling in multiple directions every working hour of the day.

The editor of *Bike SA*, Simon Fourie, contacted me and we met for a chat about my trip. He arrived at the cottage riding a brand-new Kawasaki 450cc belt-driven machine which had been loaned for him to review; it was the first such bike in South Africa and he told me he was quite pleased with it. As we talked he made a lot of notes and got quite excited about the idea of doing a story and was talking about doing a four-page spread. Unfortunately, he later admitted that he had lost all his notes when I called him with the news that I had arrived in Cape Town, so nothing to my knowledge was actually published by *Bike SA* about the trip. However, Simon was good to me, lending me a small scrambler (a Yamaha 250cc Enduro) to run around the town on whilst my machine was away with the Suzuki servicing people and offering to put me up if I needed an escape from, as he put it, "that hippie commune"! Also he invited me to partake in his magazine's annual run, with scrambler provided, across the lion-infested Kalahari to the Namib Desert Park in South West Africa (now Namibia), where the world's tallest sand dunes lie, over 400m in height. One of my life's regrets is that I did not take him up on this generous offer due to the necessity of finding a job.

Just close to the village was the old spoil heaps from the Crown Mines. They rose upwards of 150ft and were too tempting to be ignored now that I had a scrambler. Great fun was had by me and my hosts as we battled to try to get to the top and, despite many failures – scrambling on loose spoil is not for the faint-hearted – eventually I managed to do it, for a marvellous view over the reef.

Having spent five days in town, a familiar itch overcame me; it was time to move on once more. After a day of battling with the dealers who Suzuki had asked to service my machine, and who had had possession of it for the past few days, I was able to get them to perform a very sketchy service. They had absolutely no interest in my trip, merely seeing the work as just another job. Finally, I got the machine back one and a half days late and there and then decided to ride on down to Natal to see Sandy.

It was 3pm on an overcast afternoon as I weaved through the factories and mine dumps south of Johannesburg and finally reached open countryside once more. The bike was not performing well despite its service, but I put it down to the altitude of the High Veld (up to 9000ft in places).

On approaching the Drakensberg mountains, rain and mist obscured visibility and made the going most uncomfortable, this was also very annoying as I very much wanted to see this range having heard a lot about them and how good they were for hiking. Dusk came down and I realised I was still two hours' ride away from Howick; I pulled over by a small hotel for hot coffee and to ring Sandy to report my progress. It was 10.30pm when I found myself at Sandy's pretty little rondavel cottage just off the centre of the village of Howick Falls. It was again a moment of great excitement for me and another feeling of having arrived. Sandy was really pleased to see me and toasted me with a plentiful supply of his home-made apricot brandy whilst I related my adventures to him into the early hours of morning. He insisted that I make myself at home and stay for as long as I wished, hospitality I was most grateful for and shall always remember.

Morning after arrival at Sandy's rondavel

Bike and Judy at Sandy's

Sandy, Judy, Bruce and me

Natal was a lovely province of South Africa; this part was full of green rolling hills dominated by the mighty escarpment of the Drakensberg. Howick village was also pretty with an old 1900s-style post office and a few small shops. It was famous for the Howick Falls where the Umgeni River plunges spectacularly 100m vertically down a cliff cut into the rock strata into a spectacular gorge.

The *Natal Witness* soon latched onto my presence and came up to Howick from Pietermaritzburg to interview and take some photographs of me and the bike by the falls. However, the article in the paper was highly inaccurate; the journalist had obviously forgotten half of what I had said and decided to ad lib; supposedly I had been thrown into jail and had also travelled across Angola (then a war zone). To this day I remain suspicious of journalists as in my experience they tend to put their own spin on things. The *Natal Mercury*, Durban's main morning newspaper, also invited me to an interview and the story they published was much more accurate and professionally written, but the photos were not quite up to scratch.

At Howick Falls

medical director of New Jersey Blood...

27 000 km through Africa on motorcycle

'Just got idea and put it into practice,' says Mike

Mercury Reporter

MIKE Howard-Kyan, 26-year-old British estate agent, arrived happy but travel-weary in Durban yesterday after travelling 27 000 km across the length and breadth of Africa on his beat-up 250 motorcycle — a trip he believes is a world record.

'Many people come down Africa by motorbike, but I've not heard of anyone else having done the trip in six months on an ordinary road-bike and crossing the Continent both north to south and east to west,' said Mike.

And the reason for his trip?

'No reason really. I just got the idea and put it into action. I couldn't think of anything more exciting to do,' he grinned.

He left his home town Bath on May 1, rode through France and Spain and then took a ferry across to Morocco. After that came Algeria, Niger, Nigeria and the Cameroons on the West Coast — where he had his worse experience.

Drunk cop

'After my third puncture in one day I decided to turn back to Yaounde when I was flagged down by a drunk cop who demanded to see my passport. He said he had never heard of the border post I had come through and accused me of being a spy.

'He took me back to his headquarters and then what was even more frightening was that the guys there — who were quite sober — also accused me of having a forged passport and of being a spy. It was ludicrous but whenever I started to get angry they threatened to lock me up in a dark, cubby-hole type of cell,' said Mike.

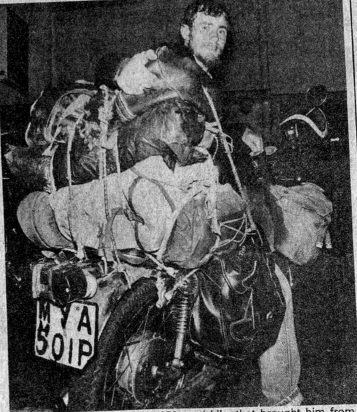

MIKE Howard-Kyan on his 250 road bike that brought him from England through Africa in six months.

After a few hours of questioning they let him go — and made him sign a long report in French — the contents of which were a mystery to him.

Zaire he regarded as the most difficult country to travel through. There was never any guarantee of petrol and few places where you could buy food.

'At one campsite I stayed in I had a nightwatchman sitting with a bow and arrow to guard me.'

During a ferry ride down the Congo River — after much trouble getting his motorcycle aboard with makeshift ramps from dock to deck — Mike was faced with a macabre sight.

'The deck was covered with dead monkeys which had been skinned and left out to dry along with masses of fish. They had been scorched black from the sun and looked just like a pile of burnt babies. And people were actually going to eat them,' said Mike.

'In Dar-es-Salaam campsite all the travellers banded together and we took turns to guard our gear all night. There was also an army chap on guard, armed with a submachine gun.'

Of the 14 countries he journeyed through Mike has no hesitation in describing Malawi as the best.

'It's really a beautiful place and the people are the happiest and most friendly I met.

Mike has mixed feelings about South Africa.

'Coming over the hill and seeing the ocean with Durban spread out in front was great, and apart from the traffic, it's a really nice place.'

And the cost of his six-month, 27 000 km trip?

'About R2 600. That includes petrol, spare parts, food and accommodation. But I've still got to get to Cape Point!'

Glenwood tunnel nears end

Mercury Reporter

WORK on the Glenwood tunnel under the Berea ridge is nearing completion and should be finished February next year wh... the tunnel will... commissioned.

This was said yesten... by Mr E Downing, dire... of Cementation, the... tractor carrying ou... work.

When the tunn... brought into use it wi... ry purified water fro... Mount Tiele Reserve... the Durban Central ar...

The work began in... tember 1979 and will... cost a total of R3 000 (... the time it is complete...

After an overnight in Durban I left in the early morning taking the south coast freeway and it was nice to be riding on a great road close to the sea; this was the beginning of the 1200 miles remaining to Cape Town.

After the first hundred miles I came to the border with Transkei and I felt very much back in Africa, with broken-down fencing to the highway, wandering pigs, cattle, horses and chickens to look out for, and villages and huts dotted all over the green hills, a real contrast to the prim and neat farmland and seaside resorts I had encountered by the roadside earlier that morning.

The highway turned inland and started to climb upwards, the landscape becoming very bare and desolate, yet on every hilltop was a small cluster of village huts, many with a pole and flag outside denoting it as a shebeen with beer available. Many of the women here were wearing brightly coloured clothes and shawls, adorned with beads and bangles and often with babies tied to their backs. I noticed that many were smoking tobacco in long thin pipes. Frequently I passed the scavenged remains of crashed vehicles left by the side of the road, abandoned perhaps as a warning to other motorists. On a lonely stretch

South coast road

of road I came across a pair of smiling old Xhosa ladies dancing by themselves with no accompanying music in the middle of the road; they looked very eerie as their faces were masked with white clay. I was later to discover that mud face packs were very popular with the Transkei people and have many symbolic and cultural meanings.

At the small town of Butterworth, 340 miles from Durban, I located with little difficulty the house of one of Sandy's cousins whom he had contacted and arranged for me to stop over with for the night. He was very welcoming but it became obvious to me that he had no understanding of the extent of my journey across Africa, unable to take in the length and duration of it as a factual thing. He could only talk about his recent holiday to Lesotho and of how much he and a friend had enjoyed the casino and the porno movies they had seen, both of these pastimes being illegal in South Africa.

From Butterworth I carried on down the N2 through the city of East London, the Ciskei and thence to Port Elisabeth, a large and ugly industrial city. The immaculate highway took me on and into the Tsitsikamma Forest where it wove magically through cool stands of mature pine and then indigenous forest; occasionally to my right were glimpses in the distance of the blue-tinted Outeniqua mountains.

It was almost dark when I crossed the Storms River bridge and followed directions to the campsite at the mouth of the Storms River in the Tsitsikamma Forest National Park. In darkness I pitched my tent on a grassy bank above some, rocks which were being relentlessly pounded by the waves of the ocean below. Dog-tired, after eating a tin of cold baked beans, I lay listening to the crashing waves until sleep overtook me. In the morning as I emerged from the tent, I could not believe the sheer beauty of the spot I was camping in, surrounded by flowering bushes, ancient trees, creepers and bushes falling down the hillside to the sea. The pounding surf was huge and explosive against the rocks below, sending high plumes of phosphorescent white spray shooting up into the dazzling blue cloudless sky.

As I planned the next stage of my journey, I decided that although Cape Town was a feasible day's ride away (365 miles), it would be necessary to complete my journey by visiting the very southernmost point of the continent at Cape Agulhas. The 'Garden' route, which I was now on, ran up and down the ancient forested gorges of the Tsitsikamma Forest and then on to the resort town Plettenberg Bay. In the Kynsna Forest I was surprised to see a "beware of the elephant" sign, the first that I had seen since Tanzania. I was later to discover that it was estimated that only three wild elephants remained of the indigenous Kynsna Forest herd; in the early days of elephant hunting they were considered to be an exceptional trophy with a very high-quality rating given to its ivory. Now in 2020 there is rumoured to be just one female matriarch left roaming free in the forest and the road sign I saw has gone.

Storms River Campsite

Storms River Campsite

Steam in use – the driver and footman gave me a good wave!

The road ran westwards past Mossel Bay and through Swellendam after which I turned off due south on a tarred highway posted for Bredasdorp. I was in farmland once more and on both sides stretched vast fields heavy with golden wheat awaiting harvest and swaying in the gentle coastal breeze. The tall grain storage towers of Bredasdorp revealed the main industry of the town. I realised that I only had another twenty-two miles to cover from here to the tip of Africa; I felt weary but elated by the prospect of achieving this penultimate goal.

Agulhas was not much of a place; located on a rocky headland it is a drab little coastal village with a smattering of holiday bungalows. The old lighthouse was in a fair state of decay and close by in a green field was the municipal campsite. An old Afrikaner and wife were caravanning where the fancy took them and they welcomed me to the field with coffee and stories of his diamond prospecting days up on the west coast of what is now Namibia.

In the morning I took Suzy right down to the spray of the breakers, to the furthest rock I could get to, and there took some photos to celebrate the occasion, perhaps no other vehicle had been further north to south in Africa!

After this I had all day ahead of me and Cape Town was just 220km away. As it turned out it was just as well I had all day, for right at the top of Houwhoek Pass, the penultimate

On the rocks at Cape Agulhas

View back to lighthouse from Agulhas rocks

climb before the descent down to the Cape flats and only 90 km to go to Cape Town, Suzy's rear tyre totally deflated. Swearing loudly, I set about repairing the puncture, which by now I could pretty much do blindfolded. An hour and a half later we were once more mobile and soon descended the very impressive Sir Lowry's Pass down to the Cape flats. The view at the top forced me to catch my breath and pull over to admire, for beyond the smooth crescent of False Bay in the blue hazy distance was the unmistakeable outline of a mountain I had always wanted to see since I first saw its photograph in a child's book two decades before, a mountain that could be none other than Table Mountain with its curious and most distinctive flat top.

Continuing down Sir Lowry's Pass, thinking with a sense of wonderment how magnificent it was that the tip of Africa could be adorned by such a jewelled crown, when blow me down the back tyre blew out one final time (possibly my fiftieth puncture!) and no more than 50km to go.

Finally, I rode into the CBD of Cape Town at 4pm on the afternoon of 1st November 1981, six months to the very day I had left Bath and some 18,333 miles ridden from home. Euphoric would be an understatement of my sense of achievement, another of the best days of my life!

Cape Argus Photo 1 – Signal Hill view to Table Mountain

Cape Argus Photo 2 – Signal Hill view to Table Mountain

Cape Argus Photo 3 – Signal Hill view to Table Mountain

Michael Howard-Kyan and Suzi.

Trans-Africa Suzi wobbles in

SIX MONTHS ago Mr Michael Howard-Kyan of Bath, England, decided to see how far his five-year-old 250 cc motorcycle could still go. This week, 29 504,5 km later, Suzi wobbled into Cape Town.

Suzi's wheels are not round anymore after the potholed dirt roads Michael, 26, travelled most of the way.

The journey took them through Britain, France, Spain, Morocco, Algeria, Cameroon, the Central African Republic, Zaire, Angola, Zambia, Tanzania, Malawi, Zimbabwe, Botswana, South Africa and many strange experiences.

In Cameroon Michael, who describes himself as a Jack-of-all-trades in the property business, was locked up and accused of being a spy. 'After about five hours the officers decided it was not in their best intersts to detain a bona fide tourist,' Michael says.

Michael says cheerfully he comes from a 'travelling family.' At the moment his father is in Pakistan, his brother in Abu-Dhabi in the Persian Gulf and his sister in Egypt.

Before he left Britain, Michael spent about R900 on luggage, a special 33 litre tank for Suzi, medical insurance and an air ticket to get him back to Britain.

During his trip he lived on the meat and rice most *places offered in Africa and the porridge and coffee he prepared on his petrol cooker. Most nights he spent under the stars.* His expense account totalled R3 600 when he reached Cape Town.

By now Suzi is on her third set of tyres but her engine is still 'doing fine.'

Michael plans to stay in Cape Town for a few months and hopes to write a book about his experience.

Suzi will be shipped back home or offered to her manufacturers for display.

Cape Argus story 4ᵗʰ November 1981

Riding Africa

EPILOGUE

I IMMEDIATELY FELL COMPLETELY IN LOVE WITH CAPE TOWN FROM THE VERY first time I glimpsed the mass of Table Mountain looming ever closer in the distance as I struggled down the N2 highway to the city. I had a premonition that I would live and work here, much more exciting to me than the prospect of just flying home for another bleak British winter. So it happened that after interviews in Johannesburg, Durban and Cape Town with offers made for all three, there was no delay in my acceptance of the post in Cape Town with Richard Ellis (an international firm of real estate brokers and valuers) working initially in their Commercial and Industrial Department leasing factories and warehouses. After the first year I became the head of their retail department and over the next three years achieved the letting of approximately a hundred shop units.

Waiting for the job to start in January I headed back to Sandy's rondavel at Howick and spent a very pleasant few weeks resting and hiking in the Drakensburg with Sandy and his friends. It was there one morning the thought occurred to me that this would be the perfect time to record a draft account of my experiences. I had kept a page-a-day diary and had been pretty religious in filling it in every evening, often under torchlight or the headlamp beam of Suzy directed at my tent! Without this record-keeping I would now, forty years on, be unable to tell my tale with anything approaching the detail I have achieved.

Over the next four years the motorcycle was used infrequently; I toured the Winelands a few times on it with friends, lent her to a best mate to commute to his office whilst his car was off the road, stripped her down to just the frame to repaint, and then one Easter rode up the west coast to Namibia. On that 2000-mile round trip I visited Fish River

204

Canyon, the deserted diamond mining town of Kolmanskop and the harbour town of Luderitz, a great last tour for Suzy.

I decided to come home to Bath in 1985. I was thirty, missing my family and ready for a change of direction in my life. We put Suzy on a trailer, towed her down to the docks and placed her inside a shipping container; it was never a thought to sell her off. She arrived c/o Pickfords back in Bath four months later. I made a couple of trips to some country pubs on her but she was a struggle to start and running pretty rough with a knocking noise which I believed to be the big ends beginning to fail.

I married Trish in 1986 who has never been a fan of motorcycles. Having trained as a nurse in Glasgow, her first case was a poor lad who lost his leg due to road rash from a motorcycle accident; despite the most painful of efforts they were unable to save his leg, which was gravely infected. So the bike was rested for the next thirty-odd years in various garages and in varying states of disassembly.

In the late 1980s I had the foresight to have the engine rebuilt by a specialist firm in Bristol, but did not achieve a start to test the overhaul. My brother-in-law, Tony, a Naval Artificer, drooled every time his eyes set sight on it so we often would banter about retirement and that we would get her on the road again, and indeed it came to pass.

In 2016 we were both retired and for the next year we would work every Tuesday on the bike doing a complete rebuild to achieve road-fit condition, but with all scars from Africa retained as far as possible. In May 2017 we passed the MOT and I have had enormous fun and nostalgia riding her around our country lanes and even as far as Cheddar Gorge. She still pulls well and produces a two-stroke engine tone seldom heard on the roads today. Being a registered historic vehicle, forty-five years old, there is no road tax to pay and after May 2017 no requirement for annual MOT testing.

Prior to restoration

Prior to restoration

Prior to restoration

Semi-stripped – note weld to frame above stand and remains of top box frame

Dirt from Africa?

Brother-in-law and chief engineer Tony pondering the next move

Rear wheel rim

Brake blocks pretty good

Frame repainted for first time in thirty-five years

NB Welds done in Africa to rear mudguard

NB Rust treated but no re-chrome so bike can tell its story

Back on the road after a thirty-year rest

1975 GT 250M – African variant!

Original V5 Registration Doc

CUSTOMERS COPY

CAR SALE INVOICE

No. 247.

SUGG BROS. LTD.
HIGH STREET GARAGE,
SHEPTON MALLET,
SOMERSET.

Tel: Shepton Mallet 2076

MORRIS WOLSEY & M.G. Dealers

SOLD TO Mr. M H Kyan. (Name)
Combe Lodge, (Address)
Church Road, VAT No. (if applicable)
Combe Down, Bath, Somt. BA2 5SL.

TAX POINT 18/9/75.
STOCK No. MC/6.
DAY BOOK FOLIO 130–3966–89
VAT. No.

PARTICULARS OF XXX Motor Cycle.
MAKE Suzuki.
COLOUR Blue.
CHASSIS No. GT250–54995.
ENGINE No. GT250–56383.
REGISTRATION No. MYA 501P.
MODEL/TYPE GT250.
UPHOLSTERY
DATE FIRST REG. 1/9/75.

	£	p	VAT RATE	£	p
BASIC PRICE	480	56			
Less 7½% Discount.	36	04			
XXXXXXXXXXXX					
	444	52			
VAT			8%	35.	56
MANUFACTURERS OPTIONAL EXTRAS					
ACCESSORIES					
DELIVERY	13	00	8%	1	04
NUMBER PLATES	2	50			20
SAFETY BELTS					
SUB TOTAL	460	02		36	80
TOTAL VAT	36	80			
TOTAL SALES PRICE	496	82			
Road Fund Licence	8	00			
ALLOWANCE PRICE	–	–			
FINAL BALANCE	504	82			

PAID CHEQ. 18.9.75 [signature]

Declaration by the buyer (except where the sale is made to a finance company in which case it must be made by the person acquiring the car from the finance company under a hire purchase or conditional sale agreement):-

I declare that I am the buyer of the car described above at the price stated above.
or
(where the car is sold to a finance company)
I acknowledge receiving delivery of the car described above.

Date 18.9.75 Signature M.S. Menard-Kyan

PART EXCHANGE MAKE
DATE FIRST REG.
LICENSED UNTIL
PURCHASE INVOICE No.
MODEL/TYPE
REG. No.
STOCK No.
DAY BOOK FOLIO

TYPE OF SUPPLY:- Retail.

TERMS STRICTLY NETT

Bike – original purchase receipt

Two essential travelling companions – originals from the trip

ACKNOWLEDGEMENTS

IN NO PARTICULAR ORDER:

PAUL HOWARD-KYAN

GRACE HOWARD-KYAN

TONY MCCALLUM

ROD NEWNHAM

SANDY MILLBANK

GEOFF CARDOZO

MARY LONG

MALIKA

AND FOR THE MANY WONDERFUL PEOPLE OF AFRICA
WHO SUPPORTED ME AND GAVE ME THE KINDNESS OF STRANGERS.

The author 2020